AF367328

HOW TO MAKE MONEY IN STOCK MARKET TRADING

HOW TO MAKE MONEY IN STOCK MARKET TRADING

Things No One Tells You About Investing in Stocks

INDRAZITH SHANTHARAJ

JAICO PUBLISHING HOUSE

Ahmedabad Bangalore Chennai
Delhi Hyderabad Kolkata Mumbai

Published by Jaico Publishing House
A-2 Jash Chambers, 7-A Sir Phirozshah Mehta Road
Fort, Mumbai - 400 001
jaicopub@jaicobooks.com
www.jaicobooks.com

© Indrazith Shantharaj

HOW TO MAKE MONEY IN STOCK MARKET TRADING
ISBN 978-93-93559-91-3

First Jaico Impression: 2023
Second Jaico Impression: 2023

No part of this book may be reproduced or utilized in
any form or by any means, electronic or
mechanical including photocopying, recording or by any
information storage and retrieval system,
without permission in writing from the publishers.

This book has been published with all reasonable efforts taken
to make the material error-free. No part of this book shall be
used, reproduced in any manner whatsoever without permission
from the author, except in case of brief quotations embodied in
critical articles and reviews.
While all attempts have been made to verify the information
provided in this publication, neither the author nor the publisher
assumes any responsibility for errors, omissions, or misuse of
the subject matter contained in the book.

Page design and layout by Inosoft Systems, Delhi

Mr. Keshav Kumar B.,
thank you for being a constant source of inspiration and
encouragement in my life. Without your unwavering support,
this book would not have been possible. Your passion, hard work,
and dedication have inspired me, and I am honored to dedicate
this book to you.

Contents

DISCLAIMER

This book is sold with the understanding that the author is not engaged in rendering legal, accounting, or any kind of advice while publishing this book. Each individual's risk appetite and expectation from the market are different.

All ideas, opinions expressed or implied herein, information, charts, or examples contained in the lessons are for informational and educational purposes only and should not be construed as a recommendation to invest and trade in the market. The author disclaims any liability, loss, or risk resulting directly or indirectly, from the use or application of any contents of the book.

Technical analysis is a study of past performance, and past performance does not guarantee future performance. Investors and traders are advised to take the services of a competent expert before making any investment or trading decision.

Acknowledgments

Many helped in the preparation of this book. I would like to thank all my trading gurus who taught me everything about trading.

All the charts used in this book have been prepared with the help of Gocharting and TradingView, and I am grateful for this.

Several traders have helped me immensely to spread awareness about my books: Chetan Kumar, Sanket Gajjar, Harneet Singh, Rajarshita, Siva Jayachandran, Abhishek Kar, Ashok Devanampriya, Aditya Todmal, Nikita Poojary, Jay (Nifty Wizard), Suny Patwal, Vinay Kumar, Abhishek Ninaniya, Nataraj Malavade, Rachit Jain, Surya Prakash Raju, Maurya Nayak and many more. More power to you guys!

I will be forever grateful to all my friends who have supported me in all my book ventures.

1

THE WORLD'S BIGGEST OPPORTUNITY MACHINE

He: *Sir, what is your native place?*

Me: *I travel a lot, but whenever I take a break from traveling, I stay in Bangalore.*

I could not see his facial expression as I lay on my stomach on a bed. He was inserting 24 tiny sharp needles into my back, one by one, for acupuncture therapy.

He: *OK, then what do you do for a living?*

I took a deep breath before answering

Me: *I wake up between 5 and 6 a.m. every day. I practice yoga for 1 hour and meditation for 30 minutes to 1 hour. Then whatever comes to my mind, I do it on that particular day.*

I am sure that by now he took me for an arrogant or crazy person. Most people end the conversation when I give this answer.

However, this situation was different. I was taking a 10-day naturopathy treatment at SDM Hospital, Udupi, and he was an intelligent doctor.

He: *Sir, could you please elaborate?*

Me: *Basically, I am a trader in the stock market. I have written some books on the stock market and have a few online courses on my website. I have also set up a few algorithm systems that take trades automatically daily. Moreover, I trade manually whenever I get time. I also love exploring new places and cultures, so I travel often.*

He: *Sir, but my uncle, a senior manager at a bank, says that the stock market is gambling. Is it true?*

Me: *Hmmm, do you follow cricket?*

He: *Yes sir.*

Me: *Do you follow IPL?*

He: *Of course, CSK is my favorite team.*

Me: *That's good. IPL is entertainment for most people. The same IPL is a serious career choice for a few youngsters, but it is also a gambling instrument for some people. So, do you think IPL is bad?*

He: *How sir? People with a gambling mindset take bets on IPL and lose money.*

Me: *Exactly! The same logic applies to the stock market. A stock market is a common place that facilitates people buying and selling shares. It is up to the people how they utilize it. They can turn it into a business or a gambling instrument.*

He: Sir, this simple example changed my perspective on the stock market and *made me understand* how people behave differently in this field. I don't know anything about the stock market and I want to explore it. Could you please provide some resources to study it?

I promised to help him learn more about the stock market. He had finished inserting all the needles into my back, asked me to relax for 20 minutes and left the table.

Most people understand that the stock market is important for a healthy economy. After all, companies raise money to finance

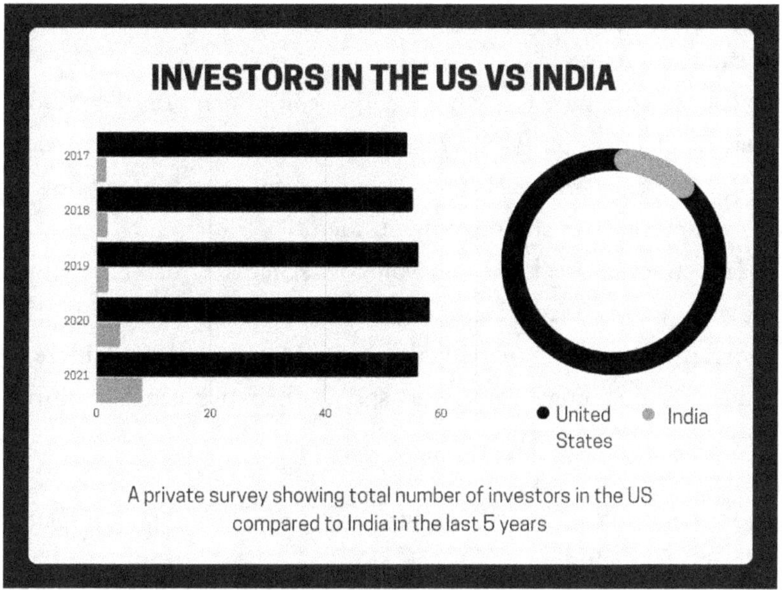

A private survey showing total number of investors in the US compared to India in the last 5 years

their operations and expansion, and investors can make a profit by buying and selling shares through it.

But there's more to it. The stock market is also a barometer of how confident businesses and consumers feel. When stocks do well, it generally means that businesses are doing well and that consumers feel optimistic about the future. That confidence can lead to even more economic activity as businesses invest more and consumers spend more.

The United States of America (USA) has a population of over 327 million people, while India has a population of over 1.3 billion people. Over 55% people in the US have invested their money in the stock market. In contrast, only 7–8% of the Indian population has invested in the stock market.

Strangely, before the 2020 coronavirus pandemic, less than 3% of the Indian population invested in the market. For various reasons, the Indian population has developed a negative opinion of the stock market.

The stock market is an essential component of the global financial landscape. It provides investors with access to a wide range of opportunities. It can be lucrative if you understand how it works and take advantage of its upsides.

Investing in stocks allows you to participate in a company's growth, and you can benefit from dividends paid out by that company. The stock market also provides exposure to different industries, enabling investors to spread their risk across multiple sectors.

Investing in the Stock Market has the Potential to Earn Higher Returns

In 2002, Basmati rice was sold anywhere between Rs 30–50 per kg in India. Now, the same Basmati rice price ranges between Rs 200–500 per kg.

If you had Rs. 1,000 in 2002, you could buy 20–33 kgs of Basmati rice. But with the same amount of money, you can buy only 2–5 kgs of Basmati rice now.

In this case, the value of Rs. 1,000 has decreased by a whopping 90%.

This is called **inflation**.

Inflation measures the rate of change of prices (or costs) for goods and services in an economy. It is typically expressed as an annualized percentage change in a price index. Some examples are consumer price index (CPI) or the producer price index (PPI).

Inflation affects economies in various ways. Most notably, it erodes the actual value of money and other related monetary items over time.

Central banks are responsible for controlling inflation by varying interest rates. But in many cases, this step is insufficient to control inflation.

Savings do not help you become rich, they only help you become poor slowly. If a common man doesn't find a way to increase the returns on his savings or investments, he will find it tough to deal with inflation.

The stock market is one of the most popular investment vehicles to help beat inflation. Over time, stocks have outperformed other investments, such as bonds and commodities.

Stocks offer potential capital gains, which becomes possible when investors make profits when they buy shares at a lower price and sell them at a higher price later.

In addition, stocks also offer potential dividend payments. Dividends are cash payments from profits made by listed companies to their shareholders. They provide investors the possibility of receiving regular income from their investment, which can help offset any losses incurred during periods of market turbulence.

While there will always be ups and downs in the stock market, over the long run, it has proven to be an effective way to grow your wealth and protect your purchasing power from inflation. If you're looking for ways to help beat inflation, investing in stocks should be a crucial part of your financial strategy.

Make Money Whether the Market Is Going Up or Down

When it comes to making money in the stock market, there are two basic approaches people can take—long or short.

When a person buys shares of a company with the expectation that the price will go up and they will profit from the eventual sale of the shares at a higher price, they are looking at it from a **long position**.

A **short position** is when a person sells shares they do not own with the hope that they can buy them back at a lower price and pocket the difference.

In India, we can't take a short position in equities. But we can opt for a short trade through futures and options.

With proper technique you can make money when the market shows an upward trend or even when it falls.

If you're trying to decide whether to go long or short on a particular stock, paying attention to the overall market conditions and the specific security in question before making your decision is essential.

OTHER ADVANTAGES OF THE STOCK MARKET

There are numerous advantages to participating in the stock market.

1. When you are associated with any business (other than the stock market), it takes a lot of time and effort to close that business based on its exit strategy.

   When you buy some shares, it is like owning some percentage of the stake in that company. If the business is not doing well or if you need money back for some reason, you can close the shares (the only exception is illiquid stocks) and get your money back.

   As a result, stock market investing provides complete flexibility for people to close their positions and take their money back.

2. Can you hire Ambani or Warren Buffett to manage your money? But when you invest your money in their company, it is similar to such highly talented people managing your money.

These people have spent their careers mastering the art of making money work for them. They have figured out how to identify and capitalize on opportunities others miss, mitigate risk, and build successful businesses.

By investing in stocks, you are essentially outsourcing your money management to some of the best minds in the business. You let them do what they do best so that you can focus on what you do best. Over time, this can lead to significant wealth accumulation.

3. Can you imagine the difficulty of running a hospital, a software company, and a bank? These three fall under different categories, and each has a different working mode. But when you buy shares of these companies, it is similar to managing these businesses simultaneously.

   You can spread your investment across different companies, industries, and sectors. Doing so diversifies your risk and provides the potential for greater returns. Stocks also react differently to events happening in the economy or within a specific industry. By investing in a variety of stocks, you can mitigate some of the risk inherent in a single investment.

2

Did You Hear These Top 10 Myths About the Stock Market?

There are many myths about the stock market. Some people believe that you have to be wealthy to invest in stocks. Others think that the stock market is a risky investment that can lead to financial ruin.

In reality, anyone can trade in the stock market, which is not as scary as some think. By understanding the myths about the stock market, you can make more informed decisions about your investments.

Below are some of the most common myths about the stock market:

1. Investing in the Stock Market Is Gambling

The most surprising thing is that many financial graduates believe that the stock market is a gambling place. However, the reality is entirely different.

A stock market is a place where people buy and sell shares of companies. It is a regulated marketplace where buyers and sellers meet to exchange ownership in publicly traded companies.

Transactions on the stock market are done through brokers, who are licensed and regulated by the government.

Gambling is when you risk money with an uncertain outcome for the chance of winning more money. Trading stocks is not gambling because you are not risking your money with a specific outcome on the possibility of making more money. When you trade stocks, you are buying and selling shares of a company to make a profit.

Some financial instruments (futures and options) are developed to provide hedging (like insurance) for investors. But most newcomers take trades in futures and options without knowing how they work and lose money.

2. Investing Is Only for Rich People

Some people believe you need to be wealthy to invest in stocks. This is not true. Many people start investing with only a small sum of money.

Besides, a few people believe that the stock market is rigged and that making money in trading for a common person is impossible. This is definitely not the case. With proper research and strategizing, anyone can make profitable trades in the stock market.

Like in any other field, there might be some malpractices in the stock market. But if you follow the index and major stocks and avoid penny stocks, you can stay profitable in this field.

There are many ways to start your journey with small capital. You can do a monthly systematic investment plan (SIP) on mutual funds, invest a little money every month on index funds, manually invest some money in the selected stocks, or manually invest some money every week on the pre-designed baskets of stocks (for example, smallcase in India).

No matter which strategy you choose, it is possible to start investing in the stock market with a small amount. So don't let a lack of capital dissuade you from taking advantage of this great opportunity!

3. All the IPOs Bring Profits

When a company decides to go public and offer shares for sale to the general public, it must do so through an initial public offering (IPO).

Most beginners believe IPOs are always profitable ventures to make profits without much effort. But IPOs come with some risks for the individual investor. Here's a look at some potential risks involved with investing in an IPO.

- Your capital will be locked for a few weeks to months (based on when you apply for the IPO).
- There is no guarantee about allocation of shares. Usually, the competition will be high, and most retail traders will get smaller allocation in most IPOs.
- The most obvious risk when buying IPO stock is that the company may not be successful, and the value of the stock may drop sharply soon after going public. For example, Zomato's listing close price was at Rs.125 (on 23 July 2021), but its price has been falling since its listing. The current price is Rs.55 (as on 9 March 2023).
- Another risk associated with IPO stocks is that they may be subject to "flipping". Flipping occurs when investors buy IPO stocks and then quickly sell them for a profit once the stock price goes up. This can cause the stock price to become artificially inflated and may lead to a sharp drop in price once the flipping stops.

Investing in IPO stocks can be risky, but it can also be rewarding if an investor gets the complete allocation of shares and the company is successful.

If you are considering investing in an IPO, be sure to do your homework first, be aware of the potential risks involved and deploy only a small portion of your capital.

4. Intraday Trading Doesn't Work, or It Is Risky

Many traders and investors say either 'intraday trading doesn't work' or 'intraday trading is risky'.

However, the reality is that intraday trading is only a type of trading in which traders have to close their position on the same day.

The market does not keep any grudge or anger towards intraday traders. If they are right, it gives them profits, and if they are wrong, it takes back their money. The market does the same thing for all types of traders.

Then why do many people complain about intraday trading? Let me explain this through a simple analogy.

Let's say you have to travel to Agra from New Delhi for some work.

The distance between New Delhi and Agra is around 250 kms.

You have three options:

Car A–This driver drives at 50 km/hour speed, so he takes 5 hours to reach Agra.

Car B–This driver drives at 80 km/hour speed, so he takes approx. 3.1 hours to reach Agra.

Car C–This driver drives at 100 km/hour speed, so he takes 2.5 hours to reach Agra.

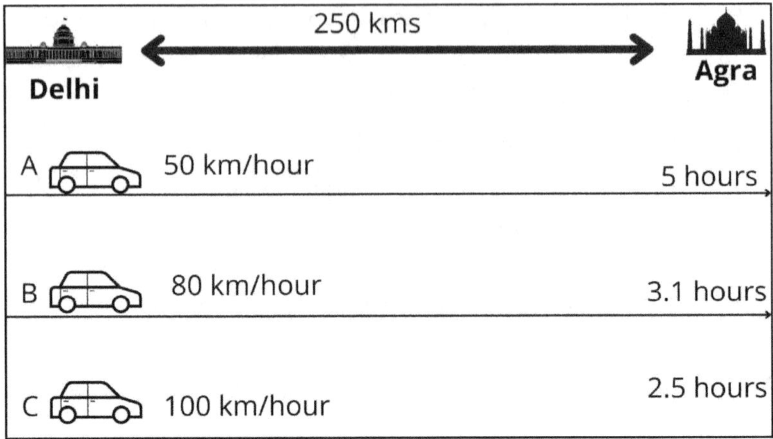

Which car do you choose?

Most people chose either car B or car C for their journey. Maybe some elders may choose car A.

Compared to car A and car B, car C carries more risk as it drives at a higher speed. But that doesn't mean both car A and car B are accident-proof. Do you agree?

All cars carry some risk. However, car C has some extra risk, but it cuts down the duration of the journey by 50% as compared to car A. One can utilize this 50% of extra time to explore Agra.

We can mitigate this additional risk with these options:

- Opt for an experienced driver.
- Start after 10 a.m. to avoid fog and mist.
- Ensure the car has airbags and other safety features.

We can apply the same logic to intraday trading as well.

It is only a type of trading that offers to make money in a short span of time. Therefore, it carries a little extra risk compared to investment and swing trading.

But we can mitigate the risk with these steps:

- **O** Increase the conviction on the trading setups.
- **O** Risk only 2–3% of the capital per trade.
- **O** Avoid trading when the market is volatile.

Finally, you can also use risk management tools, such as options hedging to help reduce the risk of your positions. Many option strategies can provide you with a way to hedge your bets and protect yourself from potential losses.

By using these methods, you can make intraday trading a much less risky proposition. You can increase your chances of success in the market by taking steps to reduce your risk.

5. Successful Traders Have a Secret Holy Grail System

One of the biggest myths about stock market trading is that successful traders have a secret 'holy grail' system.

This is not true. The majority of successful traders learn through experience and trial and error. They develop an eye for spotting market opportunities and a feel for risk management.

Below are the four parameters to achieve success in trading:

a. Trading system
b. Money management
c. Trading psychology, and
d. Flawless execution

Along with a trading system, successful traders also give importance to the remaining parameters because these parameters are equally essential to achieving success.

Most beginners only focus on the 'trading system' and fail to make money.

Let's take an example of how most beginners don't consider losing sequence seriously and how it can seriously impact the trading results.

'Losing sequence' is nothing but successive failed trades in one stretch.

SUCCESS RATE VS. LOSING SEQUENCE

Success Rate	Losing Sequence
40	14
45	12
50	10
55	9
60	8
70	6

Image 2.1: Success rate vs. losing sequence

This chart shows the losing sequence (total number of losing trades in one stretch) compared with the trading system's success rate (accuracy).

Even if you have a 50% success rate, there is a possibility of 10 losing trades in one stretch at some point.

Let's assume your trading system has a 70% success rate. It means there is a possibility of 6 losing trades in one stretch.

What happens if you risk 10% of your capital on each trade?

You lose 60% of your trading capital. Do you agree?

This highlights the importance of money management rules in trading. Successful traders never risk more than 2–3% of their capital on each trade. They will apply more rules and conditions if they plan to risk more on any trade setup.

6. High Risk = High Returns in the Stock Market

Many people believe high risk gives high returns in stock market trading. Indeed, high and quick returns always carry high risk, but that doesn't mean all the high-risk trades bring high profits.

In reality, high-risk trade opportunities carry more chances of losing as compared to winning. It requires tremendous skill, patience, and research to find high-risk trade opportunities where you can place your faith and finances.

While it's true that you can make a lot of money by taking on more risk in a trade, you can also lose a lot of money just as quickly.

So always start small, make some profits, and then increase the trading capital. If you can't make profits using Rs. 1,00,000, you will definitely be unable to make profits on Rs. 10,00,000.

7. Confirmation from Multiple Indicators Brings Profit

Some beginners believe they need to confirm their trades with multiple technical indicators to make profits. However, this is not always the case. Over-reliance on indicators can often lead to missed opportunities and poor judgment.

One should use common sense before plotting indicators on their chart.

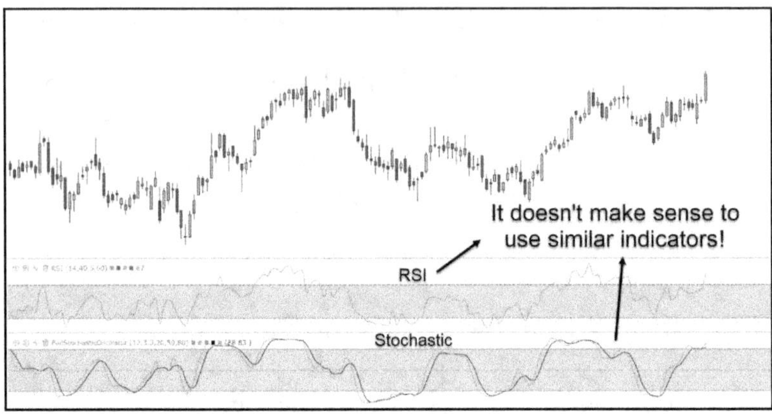

Image 2.2: Using similar indicators is not a good idea.

For example, there is no point in using both RSI and Stochastic (discussed further in Chapters 6 and 8) on charts because both fall in the oscillator category and show similar movements.

It is always a good idea to pick indicators from diverse backgrounds. For example, the above chart uses RSI and Bollinger Band.

RSI falls in the oscillator category, and Bollinger Band falls under the volatility category. Both show a breakout on the same

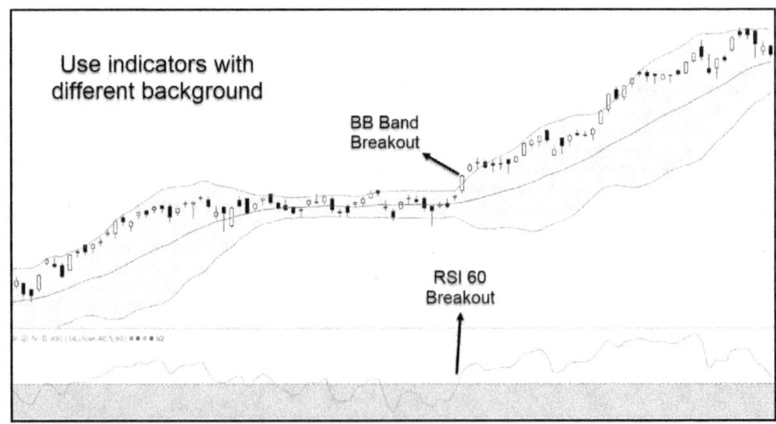

Image 2.3: Use technical indicators with different background.

day. In this way, it makes sense to use multiple indicators to spot good trade opportunities.

8. One Has to Sit in Front of the Screen from Morning to Evening

One of the biggest myths about trading is that you must sit in front of the screen all day to make profits.

This is not true, you can trade for a few hours (or even minutes) a day and still be successful.

Technology drives the current world, and we can use it to manage our trading.

Suppose you have a profitable system and need to watch the chart until it satisfies the entry criteria. We can easily avoid this by **setting an alert** on most of the charting platforms.

A dedicated person can also set up an algorithm trading system to manage the trades. The algorithm systems will handle the entry, exit, stop-loss, position sizing, and all other activities related to trading if designed and coded correctly.

9. One Needs Multiple Systems/Screens to Make Profits

It is a common misconception that traders need multiple screens and systems to make profits in the stock market (major credit goes to videos shown by the traders on Instagram).

While it is true that having multiple screens can give traders an edge by feeding more information, it is certainly not a requirement. Many successful traders only use a single screen or system to trade profitably.

Multiple screens help professional traders (scalpers, arbitrage traders, and active day traders). However, it is not a mandatory requirement to achieve success in trading.

If you are new to trading or considering entering the stock market, don't let this myth dissuade you from participating in what could be an enriching endeavor.

10. Big Traders Hunt the Stop-Loss of Small Traders

This is a highly debatable topic, even among traders. Some traders say stop-loss is common, and a few say stop-loss hunting is difficult.

But let's understand what stop-loss hunting is.

Let us assume XYZ stock broke above the 100 level, and many traders opted for the breakout trade. XYZ is trading at the 102 level now.

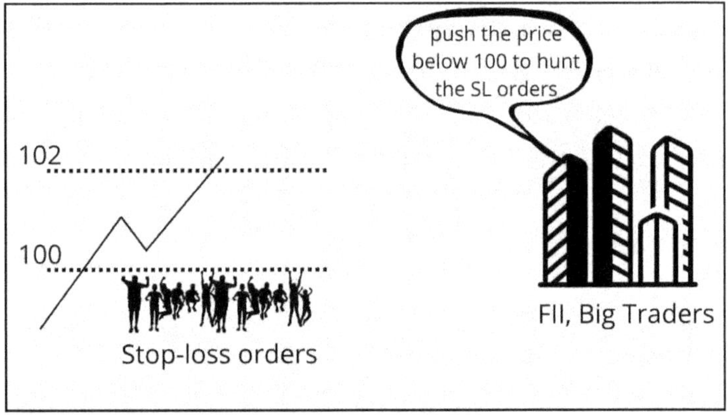

Where do you think most retail traders keep their stop-loss?

Usually, many people keep at 99.9, 99.5, or 99, as 100 is a significant number psychologically.

Now here comes the hunter (FII or any big trader) who aims to push the price below 100 so that all the stop-loss orders of the retail traders are triggered.

Then, the price will go up and these big shots will make huge profits. You will see similar examples and explanations about stop-loss hunting.

Everything looks good on paper, right?

However, we fail to see some complications in this process (faced by FIIs or big traders):

1. When they try to bring the price from 101 to 99, many buyers are sitting at 100.9, 100.5, 100.2, etc. Therefore, these people have to absorb all these buyers.
2. To absorb all these buyers, they need huge capital.
3. Let's assume they were able to bring the price down to 99 and accumulate a lot of shares (because their plan is to accumulate XYZ stock at a lesser price). Now, what if another FII or big trader has a bearish view of this stock (expects the market price to fall) and starts selling? At some point, the stop-loss hunter loses a lot of capital (if the new FII or big trader is strong).

Summary: It looks easy when we read about stop-loss hunting. But it comes with many challenges because they deal with huge capital and enormous position size.

Like us, they can't enter and exit whenever they want and they must plan ahead.

Any mistakes will cost them a lot of money. So don't worry or think about stop-loss hunting and follow your trade plan. However, you can follow the steps below to minimize the impact:

- Always avoid keeping your stop-loss at round numbers.
- Keep some cushion for your stop-loss. For example, technically, if the stop-loss is coming at 145, then keep it at 143.9 or 143.45.
- Don't risk more than 2-3% of your capital on any trade. In this case, even if it hits the stop-loss, you don't lose much.

3

Which Type of Chart Is Right for You?

Charts show the price information of securities (stocks or indices) over time. The vertical axis shows how much the price changes and the horizontal axis shows how long it took for that change to happen (time). Often, charts also show the volume of trade at that time.

In order to be successful in trading, you need to be able to read charts and understand what they are telling you. Different types of charts can be used, and each one provides a different perspective on the market.

Each chart has its own strengths and weaknesses, and a specific type of chart cannot be perfect for all situations. The most popular types of charts used in trading are candlestick charts, bar charts, line charts, and point-and-figure charts.

Line Charts

Line charts are the most basic chart type and only show the closing price for a given period. They are typically used by longer-term traders who are looking at weekly or monthly timeframes.

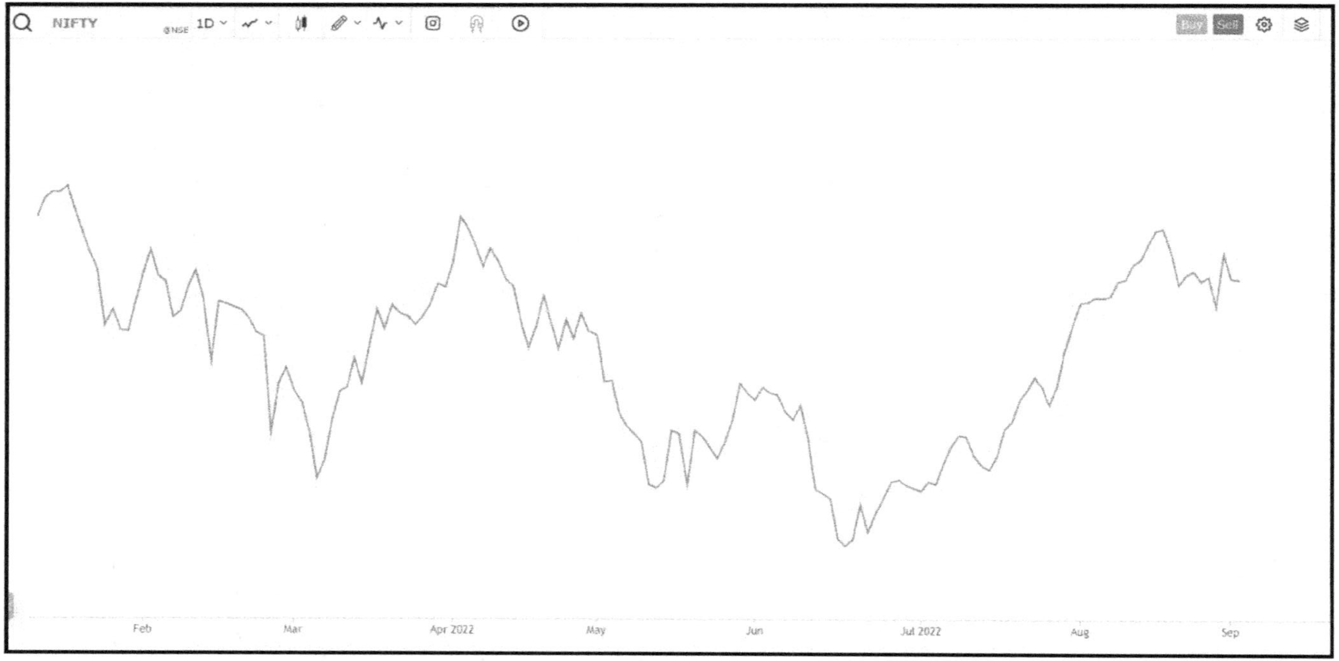

Image 3.1: Line chart in Nifty

Only the closing price is taken for the selected time period, and a line is drawn to connect all these dots.

For example, if you opt for daily timeframe charts, the closing prices of every day are taken, and a line is drawn to connect these dots.

Image 3.1 shows a line chart. A line chart's drawback is that it doesn't contain open, high, and low information.

Bar Charts

Bar charts are another popular type of chart among traders. They are similar to candlestick charts but do not provide as much information. Bar charts show the open, high, low, and close price for a given period. We can use them for trading in any timeframe, from intraday to daily, weekly, or monthly.

This chart type consists of a series of vertical grids representing the selected period's price range. Each vertical grid consists of two horizontal dashes on both the left and the right, representing the open and close price of that period respectively.

Image 3.2 shows an example of a bar chart. The vertical grid's top and bottom represent the high and low of that particular time. The small horizontal dash on the left side represents the open price, and the similar small dash on the right side represents the closing price.

Most traders used bar charts before the candlestick charts gained popularity. Some people use complete black bar charts, as shown in the image.

Some people also use a green and red combination (green bar if the closing price is above the open price and red bar if the closing price is below the open price).

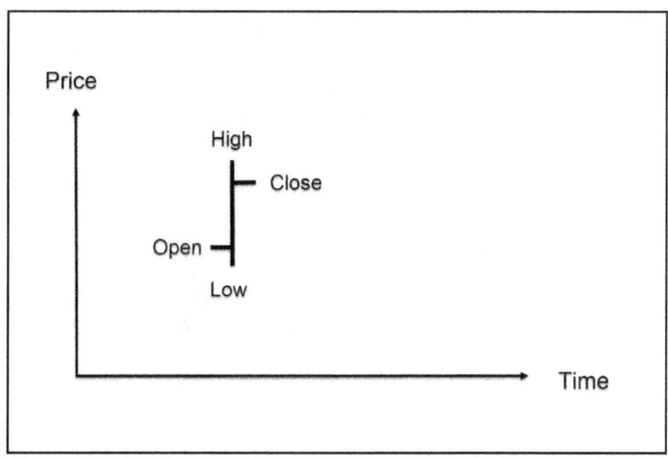

Image 3.2: Bar chart

CANDLESTICK CHARTS

Candlestick charts are by far the most popular charts used by traders. They provide a clear and concise way to visualize price action and identify potential trading opportunities. One can use candlestick charts to trade for any timeframe from intraday to daily, weekly, or monthly.

The basic structure of a candlestick is made up of a 'body' and 'shadows'. The body represents the open and close prices for a given period while the shadows show the high and low prices during that period.

When the closing price is less than the opening price, it is represented by block candlestick bodies (falling period). When the closing price is greater than the opening price, it will have hollow bodies (rising period).

Candlesticks can be either green or red, with green indicating that the close was higher than the open (a bullish candlestick) and the red indicating that the close was lower than the open (a bearish candlestick). For the sake of simplicity, this book uses black and hollow bodies.

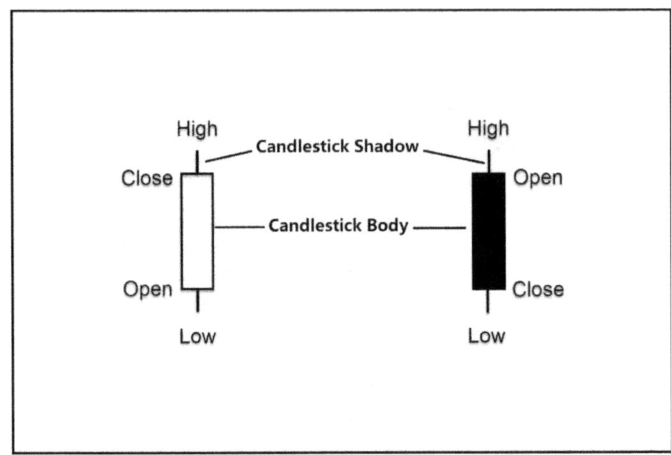

Image 3.3: Candlestick chart formation

Each candle represents one day when you opt for a 'daily' timeframe. Similarly, one can view hourly, 30-minute, or any other timeframe.

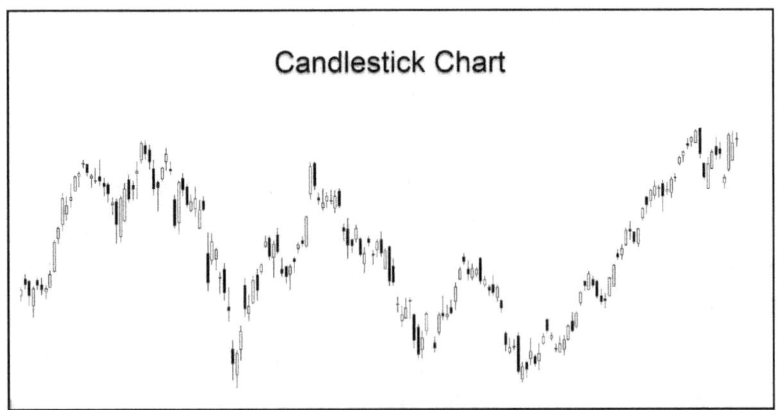

Image 3.4: Candlestick chart

RENKO CHARTS

Renko charts are a type of chart popular among traders in the commodity and Forex markets that display price movements in an easy-to-interpret bricks format.

Each brick is placed at a price that represents a specific move in price. In other words, on a Renko chart, time and volume of trade do not impact the formation of the bars or bricks; only price movement matters.

The name 'Renko' is taken from the Japanese word for bricks, 'renga'. Hundreds of years ago, Renko charts were first used by Japanese rice traders. They became popular with the western traders after Steve Nison introduced them in his book, *Japanese Candlestick Charting Techniques* (1991).

There are two key benefits that Renko charts offer traders.

First, because the price is the only factor that moves the bricks or bars, Renko charts filter out a lot of the 'noise' or insignificant price movements that can clutter up other charts, making it easier for traders to identify significant trends.

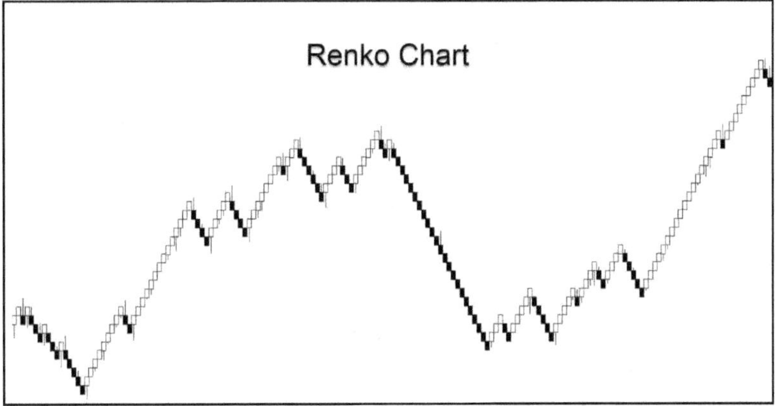

Image 3.5: Renko chart

Second, Renko charts can be used to trade in both trending and sideways markets, giving them an edge over other charts designed primarily for trending markets.

Renko chart bricks are created using a fixed brick size. For example, if a trader uses a 10-tick Renko chart, each brick will be placed at a price of 10 ticks higher or lower than the price of the last brick. If the price moves up 10 ticks, a new brick is created. If the price moves down 10 ticks, a new brick is made, and so on.

The vital step in setting up a Renko chart is analyzing and setting the size of the brick. It can be 25 points in certain stocks, 10–20 pips in the Forex (fx) market, or a dynamic value based on the Average True Range (ATR), a technical indicator.

The benefit of using a fixed brick size is that it allows traders to easily identify trends. For example, if the prices are moving higher on a Renko chart, each successive brick will be placed above the previous one.

This creates a clear visual representation of an uptrend. It's similar when prices are moving lower on a Renko chart. In that case, each successive brick will be placed below the previous one, providing a clear visual representation of a downtrend.

POINT AND FIGURE CHARTS

Point and figure charts are less popular but can be helpful for certain types of trading like trend reversal trading setups, etc.

These charts only show price movement when there is a significant price change. This makes them helpful in identifying potential support and resistance levels.

Point and figure charts can be used to trade any timeframe but are most commonly used by longer-term traders.

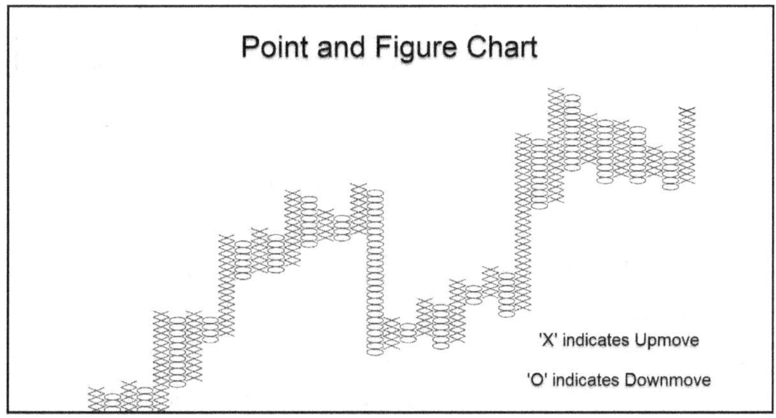

Image 3.6: Point and figure chart

If the price moves up from the initial level, this will be represented by a column of Xs. Each 'X' represents an increase in price from the initial level.

If the price moves down from the initial level, this will be represented by a column of Os. Each 'O' represents a decrease in price from the initial level.

Traders can use these charts to predict future price movements by looking for patterns in how the Xs and Os are arranged.

One of the benefits of point and figure charts is that they can be used to identify trend reversals before they happen. This is because these charts filter out all the noise and irrelevant price movement, which often confuses traders when using other charting methods.

By identifying significant support and resistance levels, traders can use point and figure charts to better time their entries and exits in the market.

No matter what chart type you use, it is important to remember that they are all just tools that show the data in different formats.

They should be used in conjunction with other forms of analysis, such as technical indicators or fundamental analysis, to make the best possible trading decisions.

Every chart type has its own advantages and disadvantages. Candlestick charts are generally considered more visually appealing and can provide more information at a glance.

However, bar charts may be easier to interpret for some traders and more suited for certain types of analysis. Trend traders prefer Renko charts, and the list goes on.

Ultimately, it is up to the individual trader to decide which type of chart best suits their needs.

4

How to Find Good Stocks Like Warren Buffett?

You are relaxing on a Sunday. Your close friend calls and asks you to meet him in the evening.

You meet him in a coffee shop. He buys you a cappuccino, and both of you start to enjoy the coffee and have some casual conversation.

Your friend recently started a new business venture and is looking for some investors to expand his business.

He knows that you have Rs. 10,00,000 in your account and asks you to invest all your savings in his business.

Will you allocate all your savings to his business?

Most of you will not invest your savings without assessing your friend's business.

Your mind considers this from four different aspects:

1. Can I trust this individual (even though he has been my friend for many years)?
2. What is the core business? Is it something I can understand and am passionate about?

3. What is the financial risk involved? Is the business venture something that has a high chance of success or is it more of a gamble?

4. How much money should I invest? Investing all the savings in one business can be risky.

And so on.

If you get all these thoughts, please pat yourself on the back and you should be happy.

But when it comes to stock market trading or investing, people throw all caution to the wind and trade or invest blindly in penny stocks.

You should know that buying shares of any stock is like owning some percentage of that company's stake.

Before investing in your friend's business, you think from all angles and then act. But when it comes to investing, you blindly deploy your capital on some penny stocks to make quick money. Does it make any sense?

How To Find Good Stocks?

When it comes to finding good stocks for investment, there are several parameters that you need to take into consideration:

- You need to have a clear understanding of your holding period, that is, the period between buying and selling the stock.

- What is your risk tolerance? How much risk (on the capital) are you willing to take on for potentially achieving higher returns?

- What is your action plan if the market goes down due to recession or any other event? Will you add more or wait until the market rises?

Once you clearly understand your investment goals and risk tolerance, you can begin researching specific stocks.

There are several resources available that can help you do this. These include going through online stock databases, financial newspapers and magazines, and even consulting a broker or financial advisor.

When researching stocks, it's essential to pay attention to many different factors, such as a company's financial stability, its history of profitability, and its future growth prospects.

There are two ways to identify good stocks for long-term investment (or multi-bagger stocks):

1. Fundamental analysis
2. Technical analysis

In order to find multi-bagger stocks using fundamental analysis and technical analysis, you will first need to understand what each type of analysis entails. Fundamental analysis examines a company's financial statements to determine its intrinsic value. In contrast, technical analysis uses past price data and market trends to predict future price movements.

Some traders have combined these factors to pick good stocks and coined the term '**Techno-funda**'. They use fundamental factors and technical analysis concepts to choose good stocks.

FUNDAMENTAL ANALYSIS

Fundamental analysis is a simple method of evaluating a security (stock) to determine its intrinsic value. Fundamental analysts seek to identify securities trading at either undervalued or overvalued prices in relation to their intrinsic value.

Several factors can be analyzed in order to determine intrinsic value. Some of the most important factors are financial statement analysis, earnings analysis, and dividend analysis.

Financial statement analysis involves taking a close look at a company's financial statements to identify any red flags or warning signs. This type of analysis can be used to identify companies that may be in financial distress or those that are being mismanaged.

Earnings analysis focuses on a company's past and future earnings power. This type of analysis is used to identify companies that may be undervalued or overvalued based on their earning potential.

Dividend analysis looks at a company's dividend history to identify trends. This type of analysis can be used to identify companies that may be about to cut their dividends or those that are likely to increase their dividends in the future.

Important Parameters Used in Fundamental Analysis

Several techniques can be used to carry out fundamental analysis, but the most common approach is financial statement analysis. This involves looking at a company's balance sheet, income statement, and cash flow statement in order to get an idea of its financial health and prospects.

Some of the important parameters used in the fundamental analysis are mentioned below.

Earnings Per Share (EPS)

One of the most important things to look at when carrying out a fundamental analysis is a company's earnings per share (EPS).

This is a measure of how much profit each share of the company's stock represents and is, therefore, a good indicator of its overall profitability.

A high EPS indicates that a company is doing well and is likely to continue doing so in the future, making it a good investment.

Anyone can calculate the EPS of a stock by dividing the total profit by the number of outstanding shares. For example, if the company reports a profit of Rs 250 crore and there are Rs 100 crore shares, then the EPS is 3.50.

Price to Earnings Ratio (P/E Ratio)

Another essential factor to consider when conducting fundamental analysis is the company's price-to-earnings (P/E) ratio.

This measures the amount investors are willing to pay for every dollar of the company's earnings and can indicate whether a stock is overpriced or underpriced.

A high P/E ratio indicates that investors believe that a company has good prospects and are willing to pay more for its shares.

A low P/E ratio, on the other hand, may indicate that a stock is undervalued and could be worth buying.

We can calculate the P/E ratio by dividing the current price (per share) (CMP) of the stock by the company's earnings per share.

For example, if the CMP of a stock is Rs. 60 per share with earnings per share of Rs. 5, the P/E ratio amounts to Rs. 12 (Rs. 60 divided by Rs. 5).

Balance Sheet

The company's balance sheet is the third main financial statement that should be looked at when conducting fundamental analysis.

This shows a snapshot of the company's assets and liabilities at a particular time and can indicate its financial strength.

A company with a strong balance sheet is less likely to default on its debts and is therefore considered a safer investment.

Cash Flow

When conducting fundamental analysis, it is also important to look at a company's cash flow statement. This shows how much cash has come in and is going out of the company and can give an idea of its overall liquidity.

A company with a strong cash flow is less likely to run into financial difficulties in the future and is therefore seen as a safer investment.

Free Cash Flow (FCF) is the free leftover cash after a company has paid all its operating expenses and any expenses on the borrowed capital.

Return on Equity

Return on Equity (ROE) is a key metric used in fundamental analysis to measure a company's profitability and assess its financial health.

It tells us how much profit a company generates for every rupee of the shareholders' equity. In other words, it measures how effectively a company can generate profits from its shareholders' investments.

ROE is important because it shows how well a company can use the money that shareholders have invested to generate profits. A high ROE means the company is doing a good job generating profits and creating value for shareholders. On the other hand, a low ROE indicates that the company is not doing as well in this regard.

ROE is calculated by dividing a company's net income by its shareholders' equity. For example, if a company has a net income of Rs 100 crore and shareholders' equity of Rs 500 crore, its ROE would be 20%. As a general rule of thumb, an ROE of 15% or higher is considered good, and an ROE of 20% or higher is considered to be excellent.

One of the main limitations of using ROE is that it does not consider the company's debt levels. A company can have a high ROE even if it has a lot of debt. This is because the numerator (net income) in the ROE formula includes interest income, which will inflate the ROE figure. For this reason, looking at other financial ratios, such as the debt-to-equity ratio, when evaluating a company's financial health is important.

Debt to Equity Ratio

Debt to equity ratio (D/E) indicates the relative proportion of owners' equity and borrowed funds used to finance a company's assets. A higher D/E ratio implies more leverage and, therefore, more significant risk.

The D/E ratio can be interpreted in several ways. However, one common practice is to measure how much debt or loan a company has, compared to the amount equity shareholders have invested.

The D/E ratio can be calculated by dividing the total liabilities of a company by its shareholder equity. Total liabilities include both short-term and long-term obligations, such as bonds, loans, and leases. Shareholder equity consists of both common stock and preferred stock.

For example, let's say that Company XYZ has total liabilities of 100 crores and shareholder equity of 50 crores. This gives us a debt-to-equity ratio of 2.0 (100 crores divided by 50 crores).

A high D/E ratio indicates that a company is using leverage, which can increase its equity returns and expose it to more risk.

Suppose a company's D/E ratio is too high. In that case, it may have difficulty getting new financing or be forced to declare bankruptcy if it cannot make its interest payments.

A low D/E ratio implies that a company is financed more with equity than debt, which may mean that it is a less risky investment but also one that has the lower potential for returns.

The D/E ratio can be used in conjunction with other financial ratios to get a more complete picture of a company's financial health. For example, a high D/E ratio coupled with a low return on equity may indicate that the company is taking on too much risk.

Generally speaking, a D/E ratio below 1.0 is considered good, while a ratio above 2.0 is considered high. However, these are just general guidelines, and it is important to consider the specific circumstances of each company when making investment decisions.

The D/E ratio is a helpful tool for analyzing a company's financial health, but it should not be used in isolation. Looking at a company's financial statements and performance over time is essential to get a complete picture of its financial condition.

Promoters' Stake

A company's promoters are its most important stakeholders. They have a vested interest in the company's success and can influence its direction. Promoters often hold a significant stake in the company, which gives them voting power and control over important decisions.

Promoters can use their stake to vote on key issues such as appointing directors, approving major transactions, and changing the company's articles of association. A promoter's large stake also allows them to block takeovers and other hostile actions.

While a promoter's stake is an important part of their influence over the company, it is not the only factor. Promoters can also use their position to access information unavailable to other shareholders. They may also have personal relationships with key decision-makers, such as the CEO or board of directors.

Promoters' stakes are often used as a signal by investors when conducting fundamental analysis of stocks. A high promoters' stake indicates that the promoters believe in the company's long-term success. This can be a positive sign for investors, as it suggests that the promoters are committed to the company and are less likely to sell their shares in the short term.

On the other hand, a low promoter's stake may signal that the promoters are not confident in the company's future and are more likely to sell their shares if the price declines. This can be a red flag for investors and should be considered when making investment decisions.

Promoters' stakes can also change over time, providing insights into their confidence in the company. If promoters start reducing their stake, it may indicate that they no longer believe in the company's long-term success. On the other hand, if promoters start increasing their stake, it could signal that they are more confident in the company's future and are bullish (expect an increase in prices) on its prospects.

In short, promoters' stakes are an essential factor to consider when conducting a fundamental analysis of stocks. A high stake indicates that the promoters believe in the company's long-term success. In contrast, a low stake may signal that the promoters are not as confident in the company's future.

FUNDAMENTAL SCREENERS

When shortlisting stocks for investment, there are various factors that one needs to consider. While some investors might focus solely on the company's financials, others might also pay attention to its business model, management team, and competitive landscape.

However, the most critical factors that all investors should consider are the valuation of stocks and individual risk appetite.

Below are some of the screening techniques which offer different degrees of risk and returns:

1. Peter Lynch's Growth Stocks Model

Peter Lynch is considered one of the greatest investors of all time. He is renowned for his ability to find and invest in great companies before they become household names. His investing strategy, which he termed 'growth stocks', involves finding companies with strong fundamentals but still undervalued by the market.

Lynch's philosophy is that it is possible to beat the market by investing in great companies with room to grow. He has written extensively on his investment strategies, and his books are must-reads for any serious investor.

To find these hidden gems, Lynch recommends looking for businesses you understand that are growing rapidly. He also believes in buying shares when they are cheap and selling them when they reach their true value based on the Peter Lynch model.

Lynch's strategy has proven to be incredibly successful. Over his career, he achieved an average annual return of 29%. This outperformed the market by a wide margin and made him one of the most successful investors in history.

For Indian market conditions, we can use the below parameters:

Market Cap (Crore INR) – Greater than Rs. 500 crore

Price-to-Earnings ratio – 1 to 20

Last 3 Years CAGR – More than 8%

Annual Profit after Tax (Crore INR) – Any positive number

Last 2–3 Quarter's Revenue–Should be in incremental order

2. Dividend Stocks for Regular Payout

Investing in stocks that give good dividends is a smart way to generate regular cash payouts. Dividend stocks tend to be more stable and less volatile than the overall market. They can also supplement your income.

There are a few things to look for when searching for dividend stocks. First, you want to find companies with a history of paying and increasing dividends. This shows that the company is committed to returning money to shareholders.

Second, you want to find only good companies with strong financials. This means that the company has a strong balance sheet and is generating enough cash flow to cover its dividend payments.

Finally, you want to find companies with attractive valuations. This means that the stock is trading at a reasonable price considering its earnings power and dividend yield.

If you can find companies that meet all these criteria, then you have found some great candidates for your portfolio. Dividend stocks can provide you with a great source of income that can help you reach your financial goals.

For Indian market conditions, we can use the below parameters:

Market Cap (Crore INR) – Greater than Rs. 500 crore

Annual Profit after Tax (Crore INR) – Any positive number

Dividend Yield – More than 3%

Total Dividend Yield – Incremental order in the last 3 financial years

Free Cash Flow – Should be positive

3. Risk-Free Blue Chip Stocks

Blue chip stocks are shares of massive, well-established companies with a history of profitability and growth. These companies are leaders in their respective industries and have a track record of paying decent dividends to shareholders.

There are a few reasons why investing in blue chip stocks can be a good idea:

1. These companies are typically large and well-established and tend to be less volatile than other stocks. This means less risk in investing in blue chip stocks, and you are more likely to see steady growth in your investment over time.
2. Blue chip stocks tend to pay dividends. This can provide you with a source of income, even if the stock price doesn't go up.
3. These companies are typically leaders in their industries; they often have the power and contacts to capture new opportunities. This means there is potential for capital gains on your investment.

Of course, some risks are also associated with investing in blue chip stocks. Because these companies are typically large and well-established, they may not be as agile as smaller companies. They may be slow to respond to changes in the marketplace.

However, overall, investing in blue chip stocks can be an excellent way to grow your portfolio and generate income. These type of stocks are a good option if you are looking for a solid investment with low risk.

For Indian market conditions, we can use the below parameters:

Market Cap (Crore INR)–Greater than Rs. 20,000 crore

Last 3 Years CAGR–More than 5%

Return on Equity–More than 20%

Price-to-Earnings ratio–1 to 20

Source: https://economictimes.indiatimes.com/markets/stocks/stock-screener/ATTRACTIVE_BLUECHIPS

TECHNICAL ANALYSIS

Technical analysis is a technique used in trading to predict future market behavior by studying past market data, primarily price and volume.

Technical analysts believe that all relevant information is reflected in the price and that price action contains clues to future market behavior.

Many techniques can be used in technical analysis. Some of the most common methods include studying charts, using technical indicators, and tracking market sentiment.

Charts are often used to identify price trends and support or resistance levels, while technical indicators can be used to generate buy and sell signals. Market sentiment can be gauged by observing changes in the amount of buying or selling pressure in the market.

Technical analysis is not an exact science, and there is no perfect way to do it. However, when using a combination of techniques and keeping an open mind, technical analysis can be a valuable tool for traders in predicting future market behavior.

We will cover many more aspects of technical analysis in the subsequent chapters. However, this chapter covers Dow Theory, which is used to pick multi-bagger stocks for the long term.

How to Use Dow Theory to Pick Multi-Bagger Stocks?

Dow Theory is a market theory named after Charles Dow, the first editor of *The Wall Street Journal* and the founder of Dow Jones & Company.

The theory states that the market is moved by two forces: primary trends and secondary movements.

Primary trends are long-term, persistent directional movements in the market. In contrast, secondary movements are short-term, reactionary pull-backs from the primary trend.

For a primary trend to be valid, it must satisfy three conditions:

1. It must be **directional**–Prices must move in a sustained direction (upwards or downwards).
2. It must be **significant**–The price movement must be large enough to warrant attention.
3. It must be **durable**–The price movement must be persistent, lasting for weeks or months.

Dow Theory is one of the most commonly used theories in technical analysis and is still relevant today.

This theory can be used to identify market trends, generate trading signals, and set target prices.

While the theory is not perfect, it remains a valuable tool for technical analysts.

As per Dow Theory, entire price movements can be divided into three types.

These three types are:

1. Uptrend,
2. Downtrend, and
3. Sideways trend

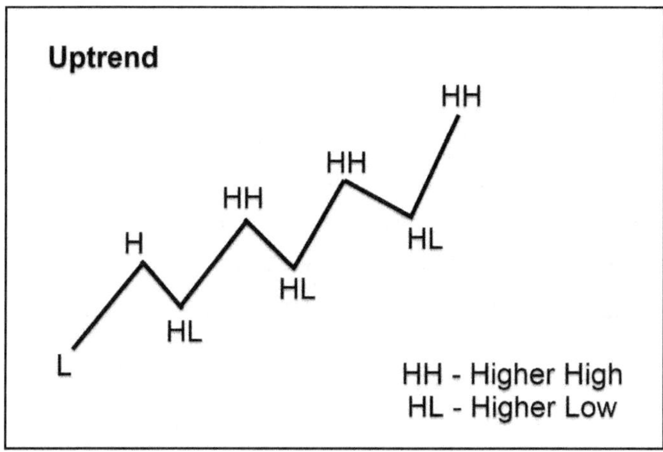

Image 4.1: Uptrend pattern

Uptrend

An uptrend consists of a continuation of higher lows (HL) and higher highs (HH), as shown in image 4.1. In simple words, we can say the price is in an uptrend until it keeps making HL and HH.

Image 4.2 shows an example of an uptrend in the nifty chart. It continuously made higher highs and higher lows.

Image 4.2: Uptrend example in Nifty

Downtrend

A downtrend consists of continuous lower lows (LL) and lower highs (LH), as shown in image 4.3. In simple words, we can say the price is in a downtrend until it keeps making LL and LH.

Image 4.4 shows an example of a downtrend in the Nifty chart. It continuously made lower highs and lower lows.

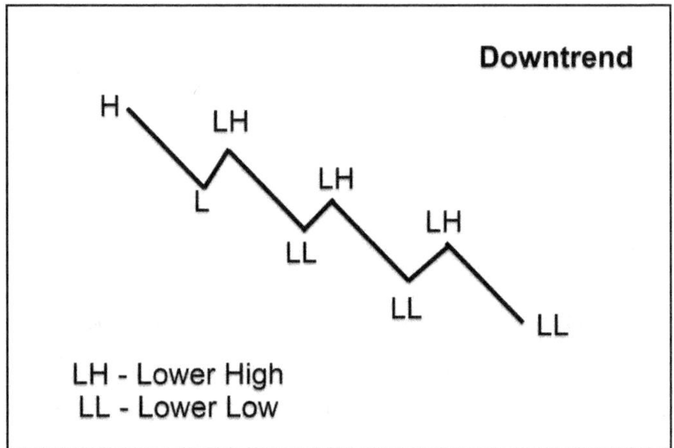

Image 4.3: Downtrend pattern

Image 4.4: Downtrend in Nifty

Sideways Trend

When the price makes the same lows and the same highs, it can be recognized as a sideways trend.

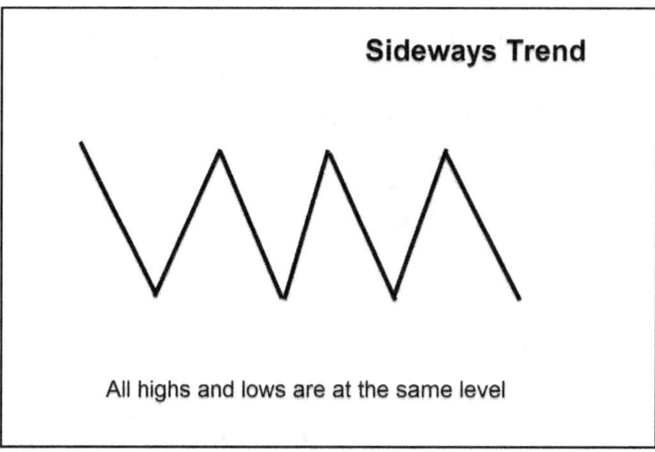

Image 4.5: Sideways trend

Image 4.6 shows an example of a sideways trend in the Nifty chart. It continuously made the same highs and same lows.

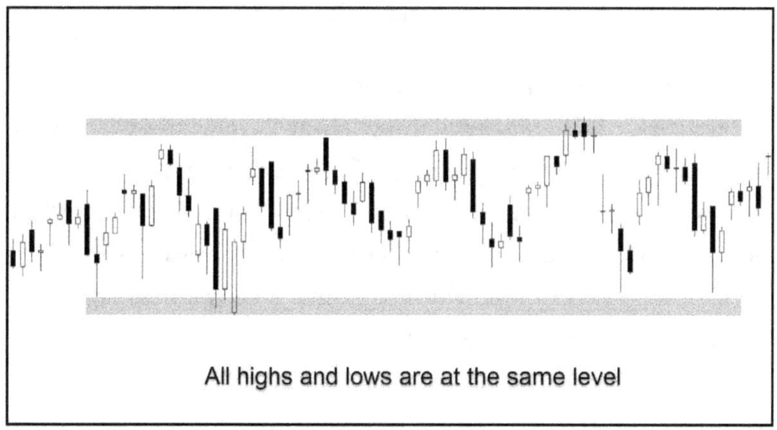

Image 4.6: Sideways trend in Nifty

How to identify the change in trends?

To pick multi-baggers at an early stage, one has to take entry at the beginning of the uptrend and plan to exit at the beginning of the downtrend.

Dow Theory helps us to locate these market turns with ease.

As shown in image 4.7, at some point, the price stops forming lower lows (LL) and forms a higher low (HL) (point 1).

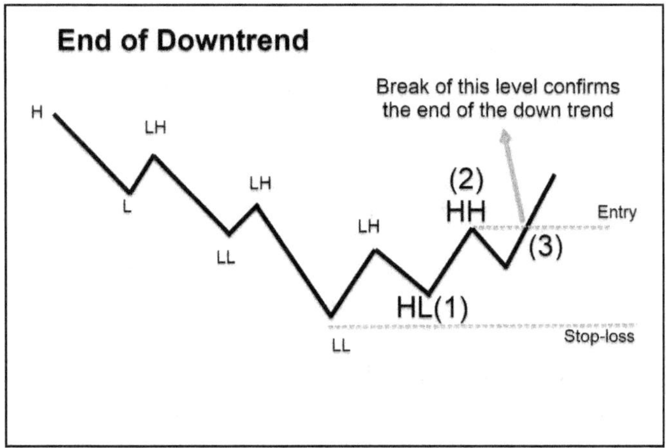

Image 4.7: End of downtrend

Then the price makes a higher high (point 2).

The break of the higher high (or point 2) indicates the end of the downtrend and the beginning of the new uptrend (point 3).

As shown in the image, one can invest when point 3 forms on the chart and maintain a strict stop-loss with the last lower-low.

We should aim to hold the stock until it shows the end of the uptrend, as explained below.

Only 'entry' and 'exit' decide the fate of your investment decisions, irrespective of your experience, qualification, and reputation.

Knowing the right 'exit' point is always better to take more profits. The end of the uptrend provides a good 'exit' point.

As shown in image 4.8, the price stops forming higher highs (HH) and forms a lower high (point 1).

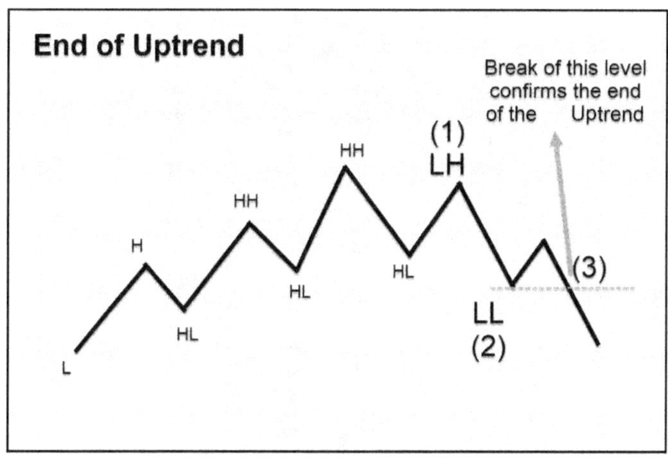

Image 4.8: End of uptrend

Then it makes a lower low (point 2).

The break of this lower low (or point 2) indicates the end of the uptrend. So, if we have any holdings, we should sell these stocks if they show this pattern.

Let us see some multi-bagger stocks and their price behavior before and after they become multi-baggers.

Example 1: Shilpa Medicare

Shilpa Medicare (SHILPAMED) was trading at around 70 in December 2011.

It displayed a 1-2-3 formation (end of downtrend), and the price broke above point 3 in May 2012. This is our entry point.

Image 4.9: Shilpa Medicare entry

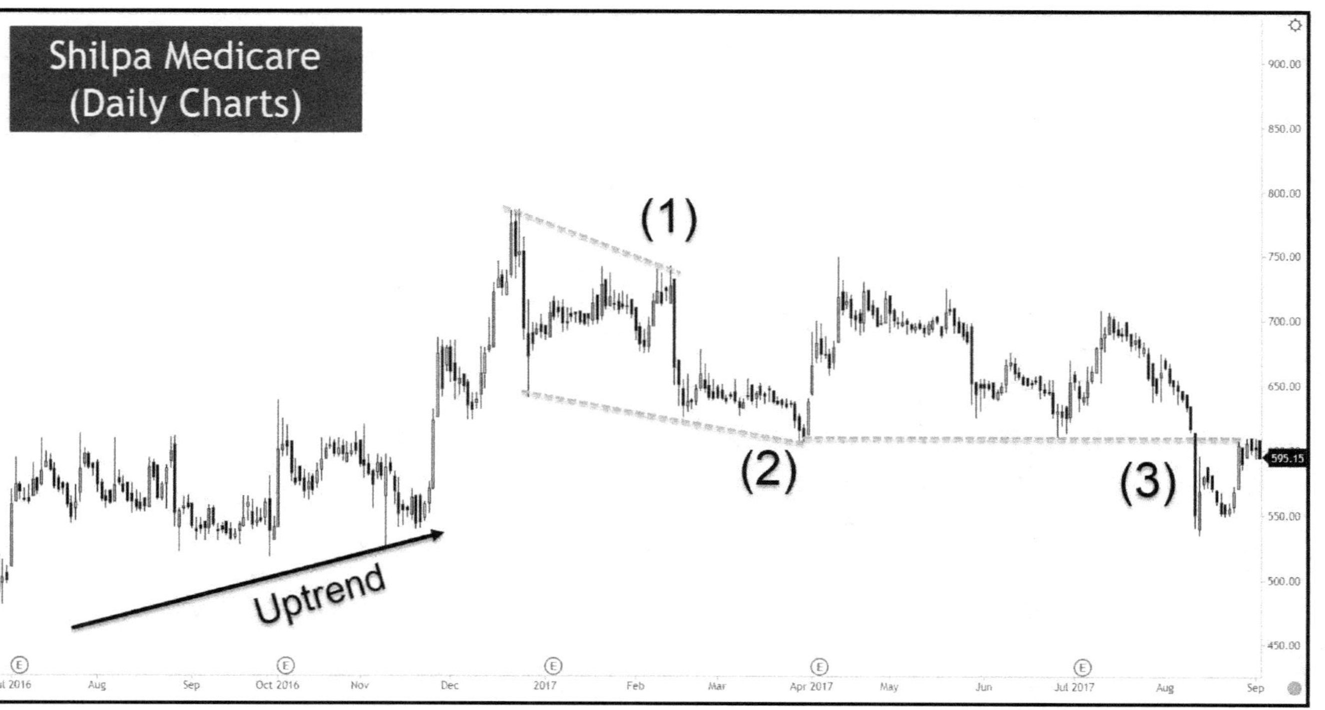

Image 4.10: Shilpa Medicare exit

Later it rose to 780 levels.

Between February and August 2017, it displayed end of uptrend formation. We need to exit when the price breaks below point 3.

The entry price is 125.

The exit price is 610.

It means it gives close to 500% returns in 5 years!

Note: If you face difficulty identifying these patterns on daily charts, switch to the 'weekly' timeframe. It cuts down all the noise.

We will use a weekly timeframe for the next few charts.

Example 2: Auro Pharma

Auro Pharma was trading around 40-50 during August 2012.

It displayed a 1-2-3 formation (end of downtrend), and the price broke above point 3 in October 2013. This is our entry point.

Later it rose to 1050 levels.

It displayed end-of-uptrend formation in 2019, and we need to exit when the price breaks below point 3.

The entry price is 100.

The exit price is 520.

It made a high of over 1050 levels. Still, the exit point came to around 520, which is still over 500% returns in 6 years!

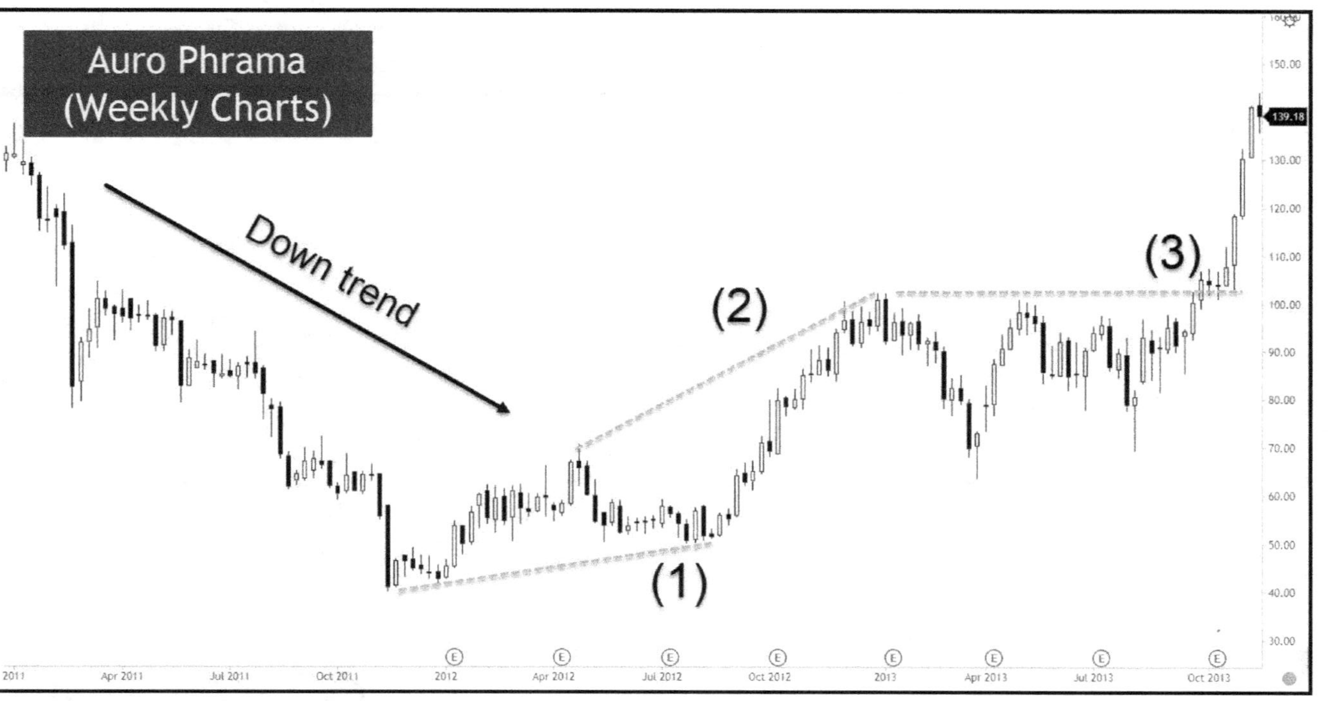

Image 4.11: Auro Pharma entry

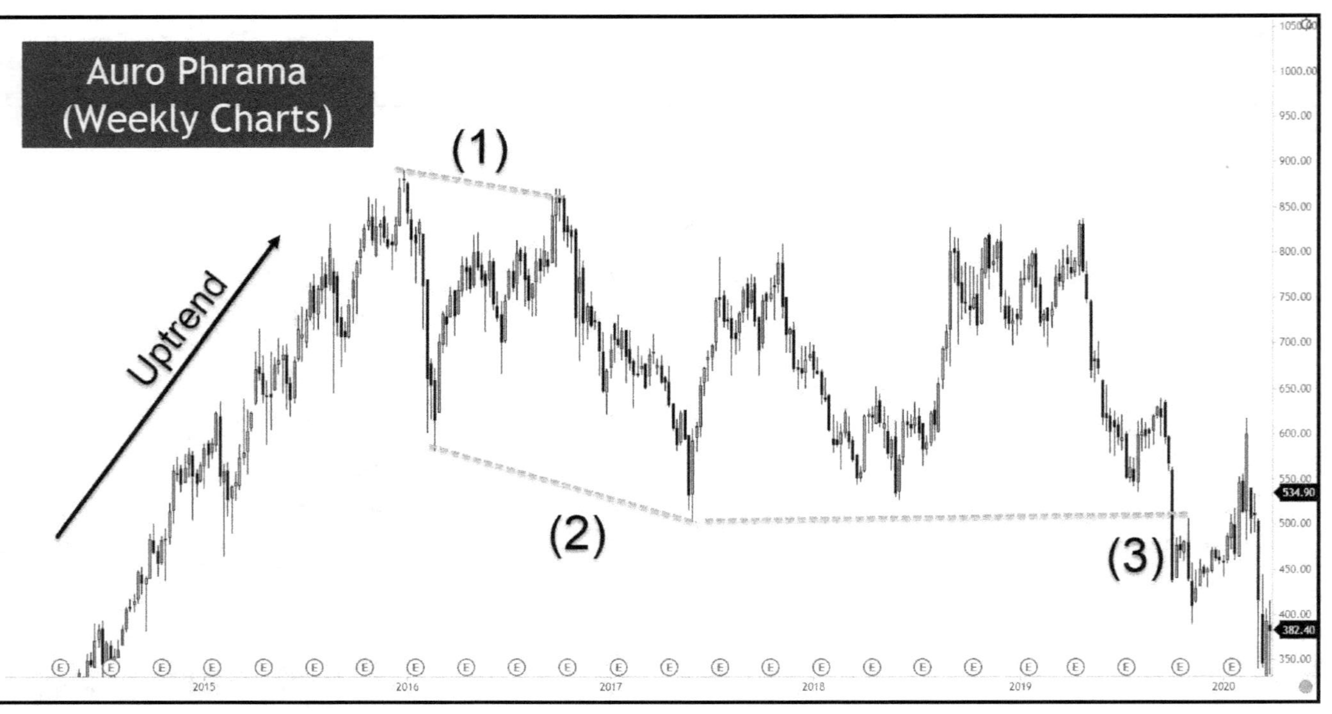

Image 4.12: Auro Pharma exit

Example 3: Nahar Spinning Mills

Nahar Spinning Mills was trading around 25–35 during July 2020.

It displayed a 1-2-3 formation (end of downtrend), and the price broke above point 3 in October 2020. This is our entry point.

Later it made an all-time high of 690 levels.

It displayed the end of uptrend formation in 2022, and we need to exit when the price breaks below point 3.

The entry price is 42.

The exit price is 400.

It made a high of over 690 levels. Still, the exit point came to around 400, which is still close to 1000% returns in 2 years!

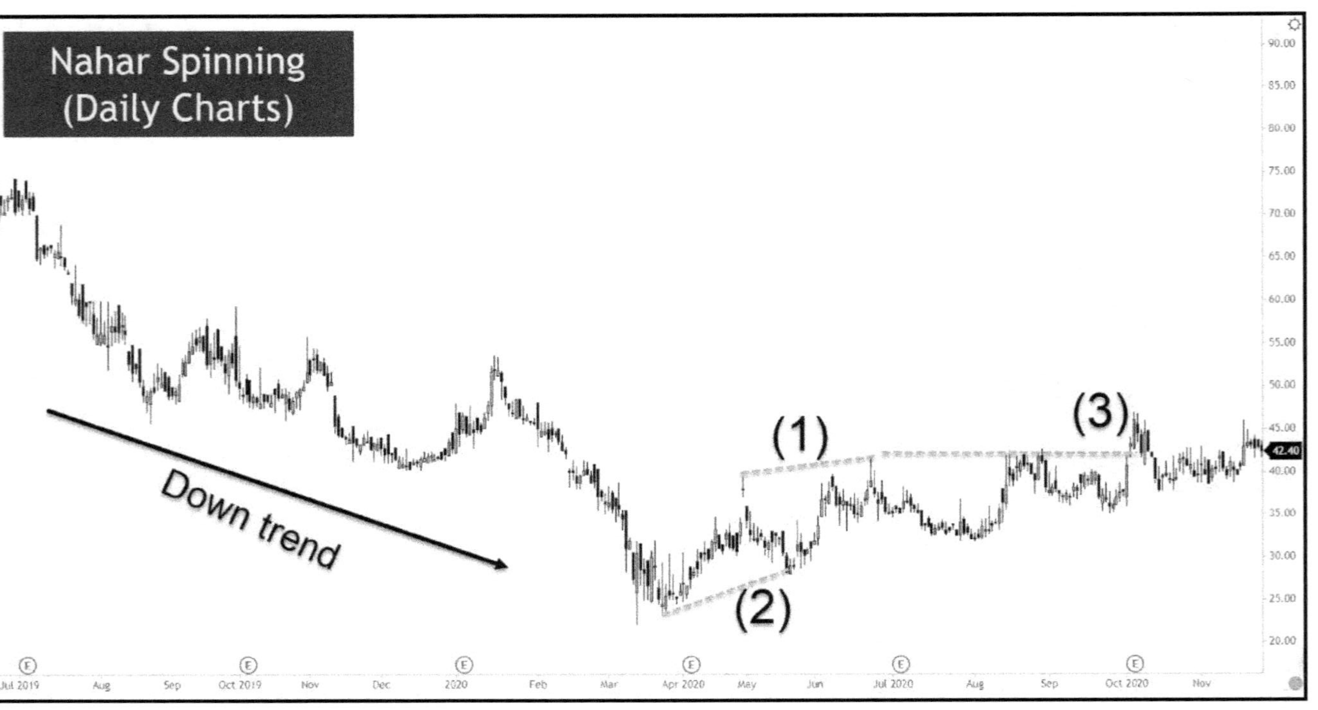

Image 4.13: Nahar Spinning Mills entry

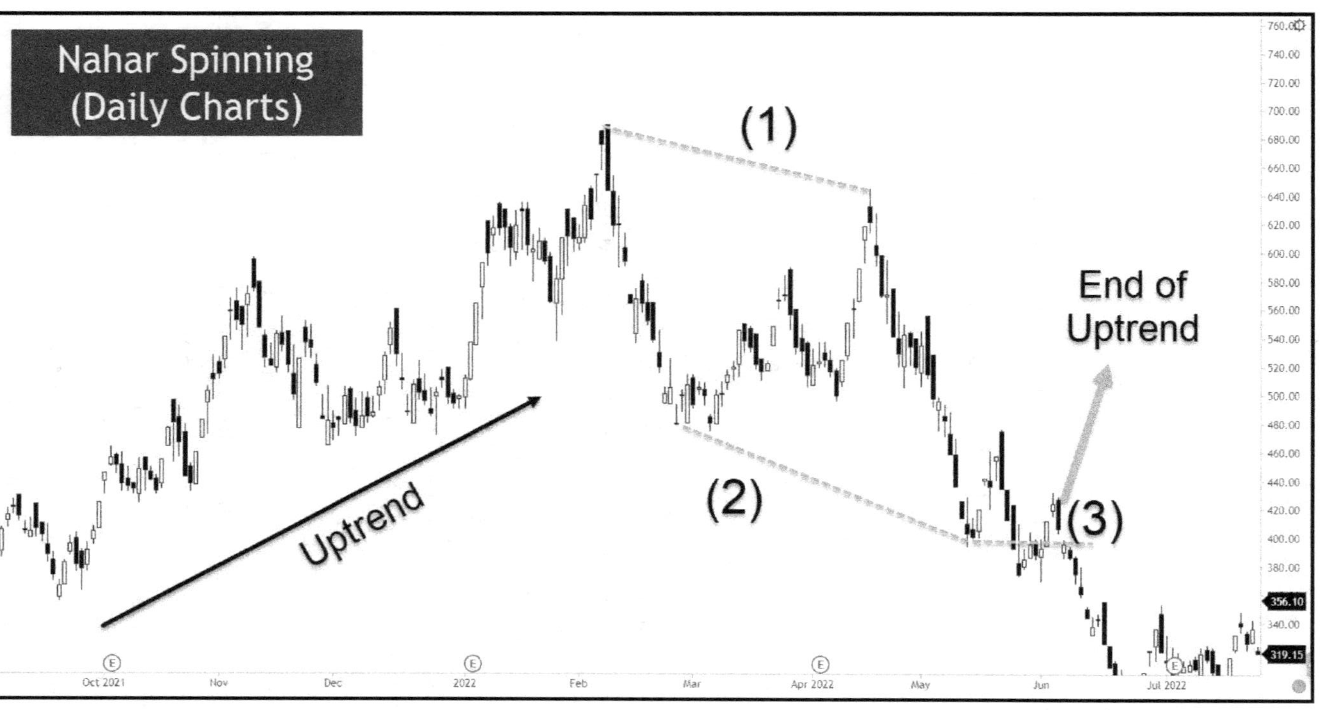

Image 4.14: Nahar Spinning Mills exit

5

Here's What No One Tells You About Types of Trading

There are varieties of trading types in the trading community. Traders identify a trading type based on many parameters—price action trading, indicator-based trading, momentum trading, and breakout trading are some of the examples.

But it is important to differentiate the trading types based on the **holding period**.

The holding period is the length of time that a trader holds a position in a security. The holding period begins on the trade date and time, which is the date and time when the trade is executed and ends on the settlement date and time, which is the date and time when the trade is settled.

The reason is simple.

If a person has the mindset to hold his position only for a few days, then learning long-term investments doesn't make sense. Because even if he makes a good entry, he will close his position soon (because of his mindset), and he will not make profits.

Similarly, if another person has the mindset to hold his position for a few months to a few years, then learning short-term trading is not a good idea. Because short-term trading indicates many 'entry' and 'exit' points in a short time, he will be confused with his position.

Based on the holding period of trade, we can identify the trading types below:

1. Scalping
2. Intraday trading
3. BTST trading
4. Swing trading or positional trading
5. Long-term trading or investments

1. SCALPING

Holding period: A few seconds to a few minutes

Scalping is a trading strategy in which a trader seeks to profit from small price changes in a security. This strategy can be applied in any market but is often employed in markets with high liquidity and low volatility, such as the forex market.

The ultimate aim of scalping is to make small but consistent profits by buying or selling a security multiple times throughout the day. Scalpers typically trade with very tight stop-losses and take-profit levels, as they want to capture only a few pips of profit at a time.

This type of trading requires quick reflexes, an ability to make split-second decisions, and a strong understanding of market liquidity and price action. While scalping can be a profitable strategy, it is also very risky and can lead to heavy losses if not managed properly.

We do not suggest scalping to beginners and intermediate-level traders.

2. Intraday Trading

Holding period: A few minutes to a few hours

Intraday trading is defined as buying and selling stocks (or futures and options contracts) within the same day. A person who engages in intraday trading is known as an intraday trader.

Intraday trading can be a very lucrative trading strategy, but it can also be a risky one. Many traders lose money each year by engaging in intraday trading without understanding the risks involved.

Successful intraday trading requires you to be able to control your emotions. Fear, greed, and hope are all emotions that can influence your trading decisions. Letting your emotions get the best of you can lead to impulsive decisions that cost you money.

It's crucial to have a trading plan and stick to it. When you have a losing trade, taking a step back and assessing what happened before making any rash decisions is essential. A simple trading plan will help you stay disciplined and prevent emotional decisions from costing you money.

Hope is an emotion that can be just as dangerous as fear or greed. When you're in a trade, it's important to remember that there is always the potential for loss. Don't let your emotions cloud your judgment and lead you to believe that you'll always make money in the market.

Intraday trading can be a very profitable trading strategy, but it can also be risky. Therefore, it is crucial to approach intraday trading cautiously and only trade with money you can afford to lose. If you are not comfortable with the risks involved, intraday trading may not suit you.

3. BTST Trading and STBT Trading

Holding period: 1–2 days

BTST stands for **buy today, sell tomorrow**.

It is a type of trading in which the trader buys shares on one day and sells them the next day. The trader hopes to profit from the difference in the price at which he buys and sells the shares.

First, traders should finalize a trading setup that gives entry and exit in BTST format (a holding period of 1–2 days).

Next, traders must find good stocks that fall under their trading setup. Usually, they use tools like a stock screener to help discover stocks that are likely to rise in price. Once they find a stock, they calculate the total number of shares to buy and execute the trade.

BTST trading can be a great way to make money in the stock market. However, it also carries some risk (due to the gap open). Only intermediate-level traders should consider this type of trading.

STBT is also similar to BTST. **STBT** stands for **sell today, buy tomorrow**. Basically, BTST is to take long trades, and STBT is to take short trades.

4. Swing Trading (Positional Trading)

Holding period: A few days to a few weeks

Usually, traders use the term 'swing trading' in different ways. Some traders refer to capturing a swing on daily charts, which results in a holding period of a few days.

Other traders refer to swing trading in hourly charts, which hold a few hours (or 1–2 days). For the sake of simplicity, we assume swing trading falls under a holding period of a few days to a few weeks.

Positional trading is a strategy where traders take active positions in the market and hold those positions for an extended period, usually for several days to weeks. Positional trading aims to capture more significant price movements over time rather than short-term price fluctuations.

Positional trading can be used in any timeframe, but it is most commonly used in longer-term (more than 6 months) timeframes such as daily or weekly charts. In order to make sound positional trade decisions, traders need to have a good understanding of technical analysis and chart patterns.

There are two main types of positional trading strategies: trend following and mean reversion. Trend following strategies aim to profit from sustained trends in the market. In contrast, mean reversion strategies seek to take advantage of temporary price anomalies by buying when an asset price is lower and selling it on the next higher bounce.

Positional trading is a popular strategy among professional traders and institutions. It can also be a profitable strategy for retail traders, but it requires patience and discipline to stick to your positions through both good and bad times in the market.

5. Long-Term Trading (Investments)

Holding period: A few months to a few years

Different investors have different investment objectives. Some investors are looking to turn a quick profit by buying and selling stocks rapidly. In contrast, others take a more long-term approach, holding on to stocks for years or even decades. Long-term investing involves more patience than short-term investing but can also be more rewarding.

There are a few key advantages to taking a long-term approach to investment:

1. Compounding returns

One of the most vital benefits of long-term investing is the power of compounding returns. When you reinvest your profits into your portfolio, you earn not only on your original investment but also on the gains from that reinvestment. Over time, this can result in exponential growth.

2. Less volatile

Another advantage of long-term trading or investing is that it can help weather the stock market's ups and downs, which can be especially helpful during periods of market volatility. When you invest for the long term, you are more likely to ride out the inevitable market corrections and come out ahead in the end.

3. Lower expenses

Long-term investors also benefit from lower expenses. You will incur transaction costs such as commissions and fees if you constantly buy and sell stocks. These costs can eat into your profits, but if you hold on to stocks for the long haul, you won't have to worry about them.

4. Simplicity

Long-term investing can also be more straightforward than short-term investing. When you buy and hold stocks for the long term, you don't have to monitor the markets and your portfolio constantly. This can save you time and energy that you can put towards other pursuits.

Of course, you should be aware of a few drawbacks to long-term investments before deciding if it's right for you.

1. Missed opportunities

One downside of long-term investing is that you may miss out on short-term opportunities. If you hold on to stocks for years or even decades, there will be periods where they underperform. However, stocks have historically outperformed other investments over the long run, so you may still come ahead even if you miss a few short-term gains.

2. Inflation risk

Another risk of long-term investing is inflation. If the prices of goods or services rise over time, the purchasing power of your investment will decline. This is why it's essential to invest in assets that have the potential to grow at least as fast as inflation. Stocks have historically been a good hedge against inflation, but there are no guarantees.

3. Market risk

One of the biggest risks of any investment is the possibility of losing value. This is especially true for stocks, which can be volatile in the short term. However, over the long term, stocks have tended to go up in value, so you may still come ahead even if there are some down years.

Despite the risks, long-term investing can be a great way to build your wealth over time. If you are patient and disciplined, you can enjoy the benefits of compounding returns and less volatile markets. Just make sure to diversify your portfolio and invest in assets that have the potential to grow in tandem with inflation.

WHICH TRADING TYPE TO CHOOSE?

Opportunity exists in all timeframes. Therefore, you need to pick a trading type that compliments your work or business.

For example, if you are completely occupied in your day job, it doesn't make sense to try scalping and intraday trading. It would be best if you learned either positional trading or investments.

Similarly, ensure the selected trading type compliments your personality. If you are not patient by nature, swing trading or investment doesn't work for you. You need to pick intraday trading or BTST trading.

Below are some of the qualities required to succeed in stock market trading. Some of the most important ones include:

1. **Deep understanding of the markets**: You need to understand the pulse of the market to become successful in stock market trading; you need to develop a deep understanding of how the financial markets work. One can use any indicator or price action to study price fluctuations.

2. **Disciplined approach**: Successful stock market traders maintain a disciplined approach to their trading. They have clear goals and a plan for achieving those goals. They stick to their plan even when things are going against them.

3. **Risk management**: Stock market trading involves risk. Successful traders know how to manage that risk through position sizing and stop-loss orders.

   Position sizing is the quantity of scrip (substitute for legal tender, usually a form of credit) one buys (or sells) in one trade. It is calculated using the formula:

$$\text{Position Size} = \text{Risk per Trade} / \text{Stop-loss}$$

4. **Patience**: Stock market trading can be a waiting game. Successful traders are patient and await the right opportunities to enter the market.

5. **Mental toughness**: Stock market trading can be mentally challenging. Successful traders have the mental toughness to stick to their plans and remain calm in the face of adversity.

These are just some qualities required to succeed in stock market trading. If you want to be successful in this field, you must develop these qualities.

6

Top 5 Technical Indicators Used in Trading

Once up on a time, there was a small village near the Himalayas. A wise man, also a sage, lived in the mountain next to the town.

In the evenings, he would conduct satsang and share valuable life lessons.

People approached him to get solutions to their problems.

Some people always asked about the same problem.

Once, the sage shared a joke before answering the questions. Everyone laughed at it.

After some time, the sage repeated the same joke. This time only some people laughed.

He repeated the same joke for the third time, and nobody laughed.

A person asked the sage, "Why are you repeating the same joke again and again?"

The sage replied with a smile, "People can't laugh at the same joke over and over. But why do all of you crib repeatedly about the same problem?"

But the irony is that most people make the same mistakes again and again in the stock market, only to lose money.

Psychological factors can play a significant role in trading, and it is vital to be aware of them to make the best decisions. Fear, greed, and hope are some of the emotions that can influence traders.

Fear can cause traders to exit positions too early or to avoid trading altogether. Greed can lead to overtrading or holding on to losing positions for too long. Hope can cloud judgment and result in bad decision-making.

It is crucial to manage these emotions and stay disciplined to succeed in trading. If you are a beginner, a clear trading plan with 1–2 indicators will bring a lot of discipline in trading and helps to avoid revenge trading (taking unnecessary trades after facing some failures).

Technical indicators are either simple or complex mathematical calculations based on historic price, volume, or open interest information that aim to forecast future market behavior. Traders can use indicators in all timeframes, from those looking for long-term investment opportunities to those who use day trading strategies. Depending on the intended purpose, many types of technical indicators are available.

There are four main categories of technical indicators: trend, momentum, volatility, and volume. Each one can be used in a different way to try and predict future market movements. Some technical indicators can be used as standalone tools. In contrast, others work best when combined with other indicators or forms of analysis.

Trend indicators give traders clues about the direction of the price. The most popular trend indicator is the moving average, which shows the average price of a security over a specific period of time. Other trend indicators include the parabolic SAR and the MACD.

Parabolic SAR (PSAR) Indicator is a technical indicator that consists of a series of dots above or below the price candles. It will appear below the price candle if the stock is in an uptrend and above the price candle if it is in a downtrend.

Moving average convergence/divergence (MACD) is a trend-following momentum indicator that shows the relationship between two exponential moving averages (EMAs) of a security's price. The MACD line is calculated by subtracting the 26-period EMA from the 12-period EMA.

Momentum indicators show how quickly the price of a security is changing. The Relative Strength Index (RSI) is the most famous momentum indicator, which measures the speed and change of price movements. Other momentum indicators include the Stochastic Oscillator and the Williams %R.

Volatility indicators show how much the price of a security has fluctuated over time. The most popular volatility indicator is the Bollinger Band, which plots two standard deviations lines above and below a simple moving average. Other volatility indicators include average true range (ATR) and standard deviation.

Volume indicators show how many shares or contracts have been traded in a security or market. The most popular volume indicator is on-balance-volume (OBV), which adds and subtracts volume based on the direction of the price. Other volume indicators include Chaikin money flow (CMF), negative volume index (NVI), and Volume Profile.

Technical indicators can be used as standalone tools or in conjunction with other technical and fundamental analysis techniques. They are one piece of information that traders use to make informed decisions about their trading strategies. When combined with other forms of analysis, technical indicators can provide valuable insights into the market and help traders identify potential trading opportunities.

1. Moving Average (MA)

A moving average indicator is a simple tool used by traders to help them make better decisions when it comes to buying and selling stocks. This indicator averages the price of a stock over a period of time (selected by the user), giving traders an idea of what the stock has been doing recently.

The period of time that is used to calculate a moving average can also impact its usefulness.

A shorter timeframe will be more responsive to recent price changes, but it can also generate more false signals.

A longer timeframe will smooth out the price action and filter out some noise, but it will also lag behind the current price action.

The most common periods for the moving average indicator are 10 days, 20 days, 50 days, 100 days, and 200 days. These time periods can be changed depending on the trader's preferences.

The 50-day and 200-day moving averages are the most popular among long-term investors. In contrast, 10-day and 20-day moving averages are more popular among short-term traders.

Types of Moving Average

Traders and investors use many moving average types and variations to track the direction of a security's price. Each type of a moving average focuses on a different metric, such as closing price, trading volume, or opening price.

The most common moving averages (MA) are the simple moving average (SMA), exponential moving average (EMA), and weighted moving average (WMA).

The simple moving average (SMA) is calculated by taking the arithmetic mean of a security's prices over a given period of time.

The SMA is considered to be a lagging indicator because it is based on past prices.

The exponential moving average (EMA) gives more weight to recent data points, which makes it more responsive to recent price changes than the SMA. The EMA is also a lagging indicator.

The weighted moving average (WMA) is similar to the exponential moving average but gives more weight to the most recent data points. The WMA is a leading indicator because it predicts future price movements.

For explanation's sake, this book uses SMA.

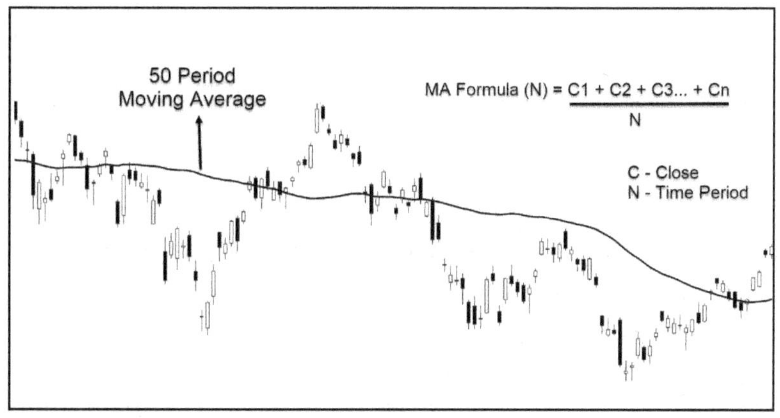

Image 6.1: Simple moving average indicator

Uses of Moving Average

We can use the moving average indicator in two different ways.

The first way is to use it as a trend-following indicator.

This means that if the stock's price is above the moving average, then the trend is considered up, and the trader would want to buy the stock.

Image 6.2 shows an example where the price is trading above the 50 SMA. The SMA slope is also headed upside. It means the trend is up.

Image 6.2: Price is above SMA

We should not buy at this point. Traders should look for buying opportunities when the price shows some pullback and takes support at the SMA level.

If the stock's price is below the moving average, then the trend is considered down, and the trader would look to sell the stock.

Image 6.3 shows an example where the price is trading below the 50 SMA. Besides, the SMA slope is also headed downside. It means the trend is down.

We should not opt for a short trade at this point. Traders should look for selling opportunities when the price shows some bounce and takes resistance at the SMA level.

The second way to use the moving average indicator is as a support and resistance level.

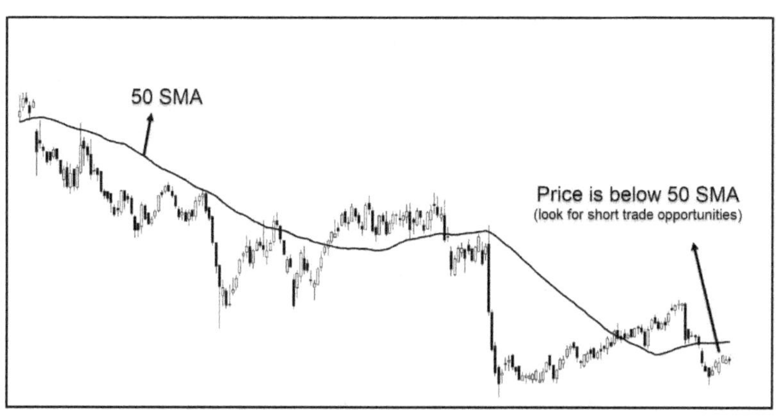

Image 6.3: Price is below SMA

Observe images 6.4 and 6.5. In both cases, the price is trading above 50 MA, and the slope of the MA is also up, indicating the stocks are in an uptrend.

Later price gave a slight pullback due to booking profits and took support precisely at the MA.

At this point, traders can opt for a long trade, keep stop-loss below the MA and try to ride the uptrend. They can also use MA as their trailing stop-loss.

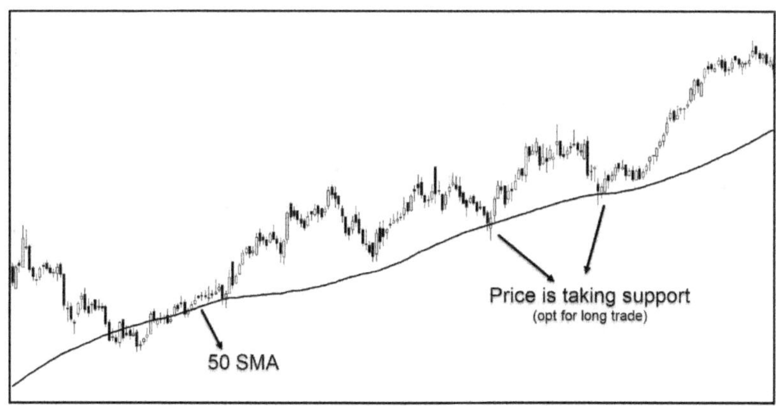

Image 6.4: Price is taking support at SMA

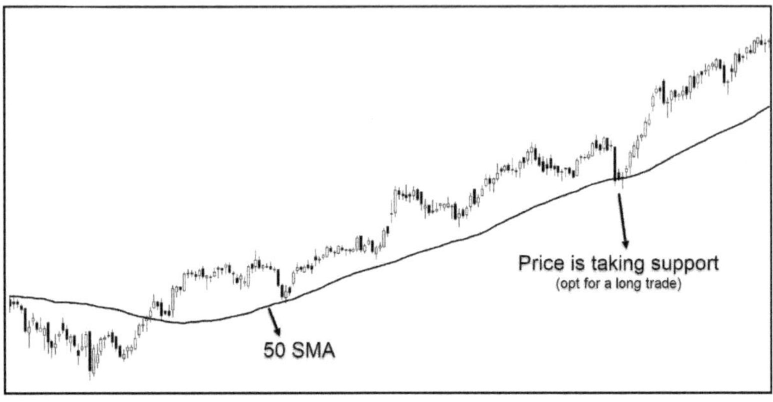

Image 6.5: Price is taking support at SMA

Observe images 6.6 and 6.7. In both cases, the price is trading below 50 MA, and the slope of the MA is also down, indicating the stocks are in a downtrend.

Later, the price slightly bounced and took resistance precisely at the MA.

At this point, traders can opt for a short trade, keep stop-loss above the MA and try to ride the downtrend. They can also use MA as their trailing stop-loss.

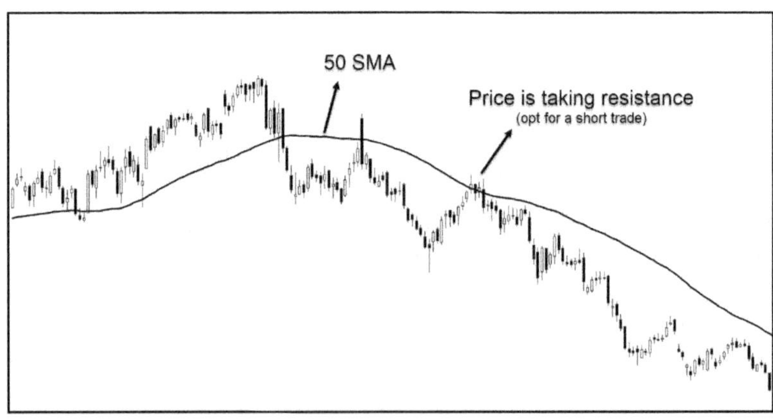

Image 6.6: Price is taking resistance at SMA

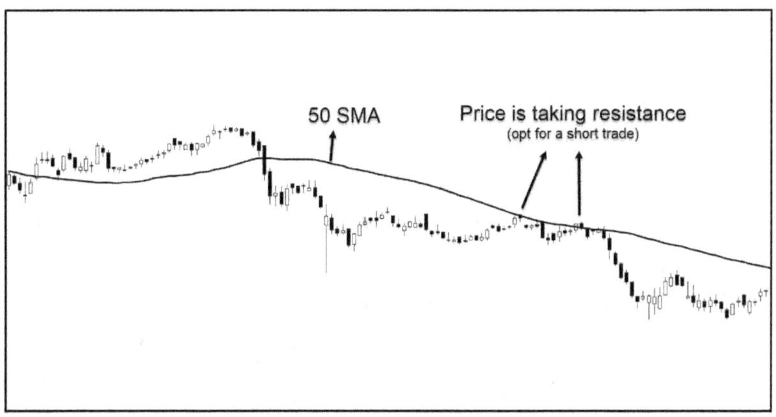

Image 6.7: Price is taking resistance at SMA

The moving average indicator can be a helpful tool for traders. Still, it is essential to remember that it is just one indicator and should not be the only thing considered when making trading decisions. A trader must complement it with other technical concepts or analysis tools to make the most informed decision possible.

Limitations

A moving average indicator is a powerful tool to identify and interpret trends in the stock market, but it also has some limitations.

1. MA tends to respond slowly to sharp price changes because it takes an average of past data. When the market experiences volatility, the indicator lags behind its movements and may not be able to inform the trader adequately.

2. It can generate duplicate signals in the sideways market. So it is always a good idea to club with any other indicator, such as average directional moving index (ADX) or RSI

(explained below), to know the strength of a trend or momentum.

2. Relative Strength Index (RSI)

The Relative Strength Index (RSI) is a simple momentum indicator that evaluates the magnitude of recent price changes to identify overbought and oversold conditions in the price of a stock.

The indicator was initially developed by J. Welles Wilder and featured in his 1978 book, *New Concepts in Technical Trading Systems*. The RSI is displayed as an oscillator and fluctuates between 0 and 100. Readings below 30 are considered oversold, while readings above 70 are considered overbought.

Like other momentum indicators, the RSI can generate buy and sell signals. A buy signal occurs when the RSI crosses below its oversold threshold (usually 30). In contrast, a sell signal occurs when it crosses above its overbought threshold (usually 70).

These signals can provide further confirmation for traders who use other technical indicators, such as moving averages or candlestick patterns, to generate their trading decisions.

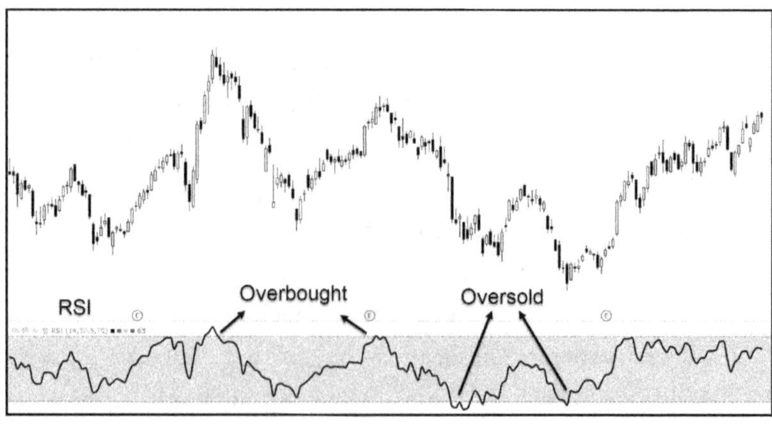

Image 6.8: RSI indicator

The RSI can also be used to identify divergences, which occur when the price of an asset is making new highs or lows while the RSI is failing to do so.

A bearish divergence occurs when the price makes a new high (while the RSI makes a lower high), signaling that momentum is shifting against the bulls.

A bullish divergence occurs when the price makes a new low (while the RSI makes a higher low), indicating that momentum is starting to turn in favor of the bulls.

Divergences can be used as leading indicators to help predict future price movements. However, it's important to note that divergences are not always reliable and should be used in conjunction with other technical indicators.

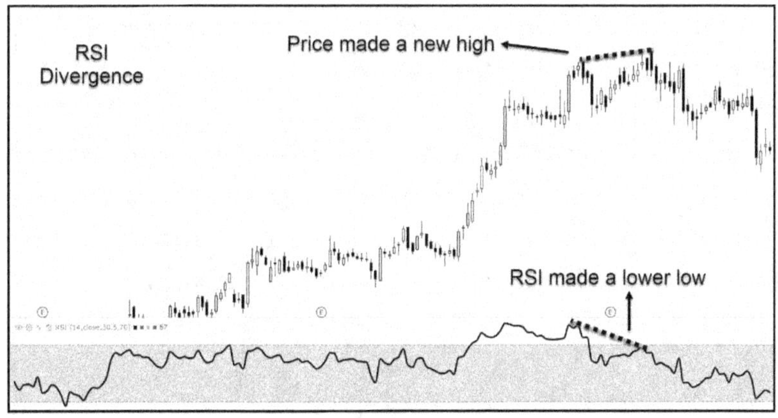

Image 6.9: RSI divergence

But the best way to use RSI is explained by John Hayden in his book *RSI–The Complete Guide*.

According to him, any RSI value greater than 60 indicates a bullish market. Any RSI level below 40 indicates a bearish market, and an RSI level between 40-60 shows a sideways market.

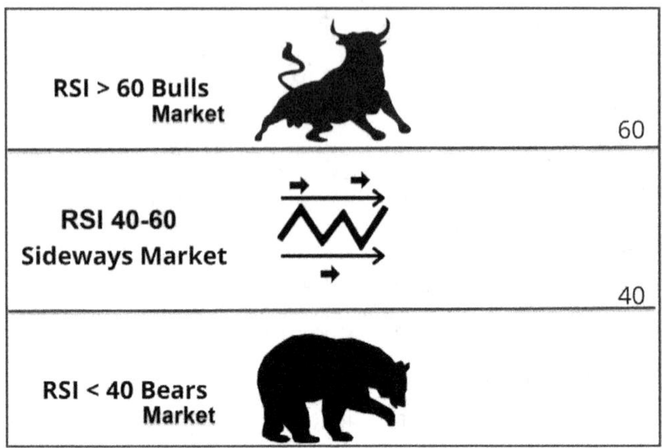

Image 6.10: RSI 40-60 rule

If you look at image 6.11, the price displayed sideways behavior whenever RSI stayed between 40-60 levels.

When the RSI value increased above 60, the price showed an uptrend; when the RSI fell below 40, the price displayed a downtrend.

The RSI is a versatile indicator that can be used in various ways. Still, it's important to remember that it is just one tool in a trader's toolbox. As with all technical indicators, the RSI should not be used in isolation but as part of a larger trading strategy.

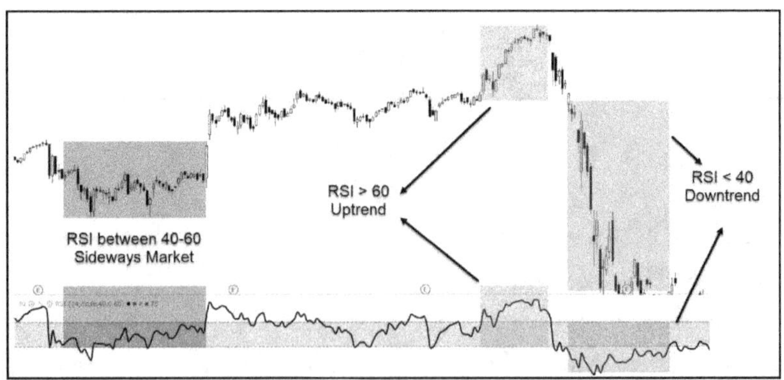

Image 6.11: Example for RSI 40-60 rule

Limitations

While RSI can be a helpful tool when trading, it's important to remember the limitations of this indicator.

1. RSI values can mislead people if the price shows sharp jumps. This is a common factor with penny stocks or stocks with less liquidity.
2. RSI can give many divergences in a strong trend. For example, it can show many bearish divergences in a strong uptrend. So, taking a short trade at this point is not a good idea.
3. It provides many fake signals in a lower timeframe. So avoid using it in lower timeframes, like 5-minutes or 10-minutes.

3. BOLLINGER BANDS

Bollinger Bands are one of the popular technical indicators that traders use to help identify potential entry and exit points.

The indicator comprises three lines: an upper line, a lower line, and a middle line. The middle line is typically a simple moving

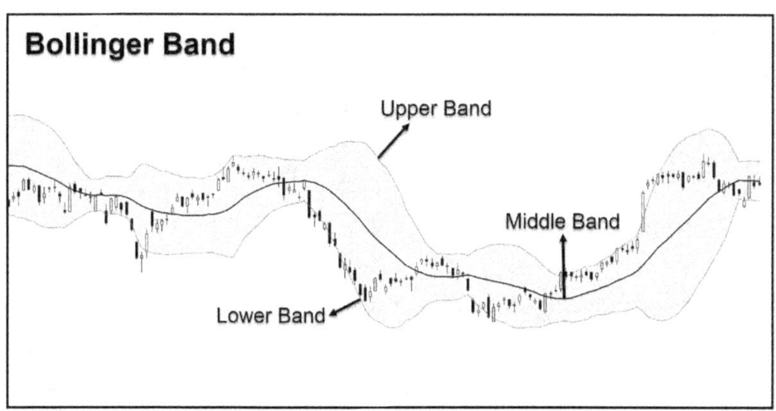

Image 6.12: Bollinger Band

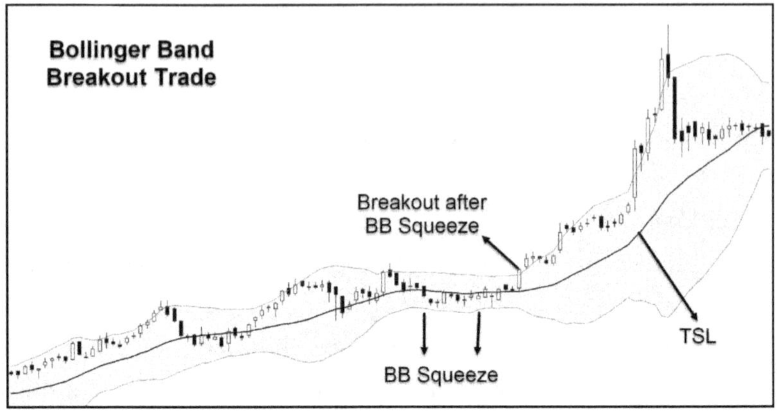

Image 6.13: Bollinger Band breakout trade

average (SMA), while the upper and lower lines are set two standard deviations above and below the middle line.

Bollinger Bands can be used on any timeframe, but they are most often used on longer-term charts like daily or weekly charts.

The main idea behind Bollinger Bands is that price tends to stay within the upper and lower bands during periods of low volatility. Still, it will break out of the bands during periods of high volatility.

When prices break out of the upper Bollinger Band after some consolidation, it is called a Bollinger Band Squeeze. Traders opt for a long trade at this time, keeping a stop-loss at the low of the breakout candle. They carry positions keeping the middle band as their trailing stop-loss.

Limitations

While Bollinger Bands can be an effective tool in helping traders make sound decisions, some limitations to Bollinger Band should be considered when utilizing the indicator for trading purposes.

1. As the values in Bollinger Bands are derived from moving averages, it might show many false signals in a sideways market.
2. Bollinger Bands can be ineffective in trading markets with low volatility as the indicator relies on changes in price action to generate signals. In such instances, other indicators may need to be used instead to identify potential buying and selling opportunities correctly.

4. Pivot Points

Pivot points are technical indicators widely used by traders to determine potential support and resistance levels in the market. By plotting these points on a chart, traders can see where the market will likely find support or resistance as prices move higher or lower.

Pivot points are calculated using the open, high, low, and close prices of a security for a given period. There are several different ways to calculate pivot points, but the five-point system is the most common.

This system uses the following formulas:

Pivot Point (PP) = (High + Low + Close) / 3

Considering Support (S) and Resistance (R)
S1 = (2 × PP) – High
S2 = PP – (High – Low)
S3 = Low – 2(High – PP)

R1 = (2 × PP) – Low
R2 = PP + (High – Low)
R3 = High + 2(PP – Low)

The pivot point is the level at which the market will likely see the most action as prices move higher or lower.

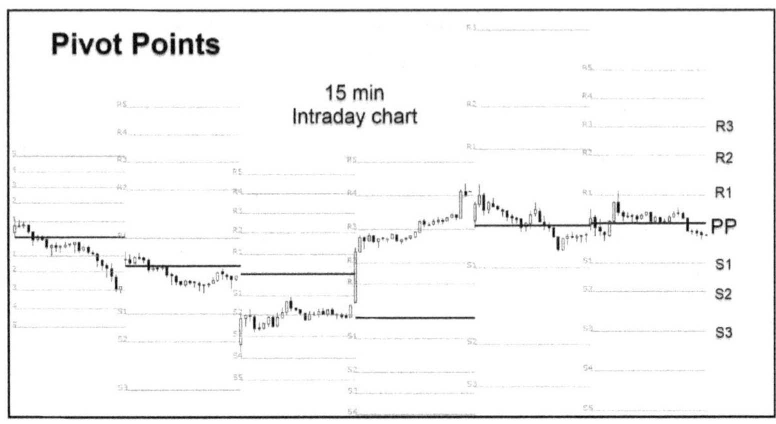

Image 6.14: Pivot points (15-minute intraday chart)

The first level of support and resistance is used to determine where the market will likely find some initial support or resistance.

The second and third levels are used to identify possible areas where the market may stall or reverse.

Intraday traders and short-term traders use pivot points extensively. Below are some of the crucial points about pivot points:

1) Pivot points will not change when you change the intraday timeframe

Pivot points remain the same irrespective of the timeframe you choose.

Image 6.15 shows the pivot point details for Bajaj Finance chart on 2 September 2022.

PP – 7222
S1 – 7109
S2 – 7030
R1 – 7301
R2 – 7413

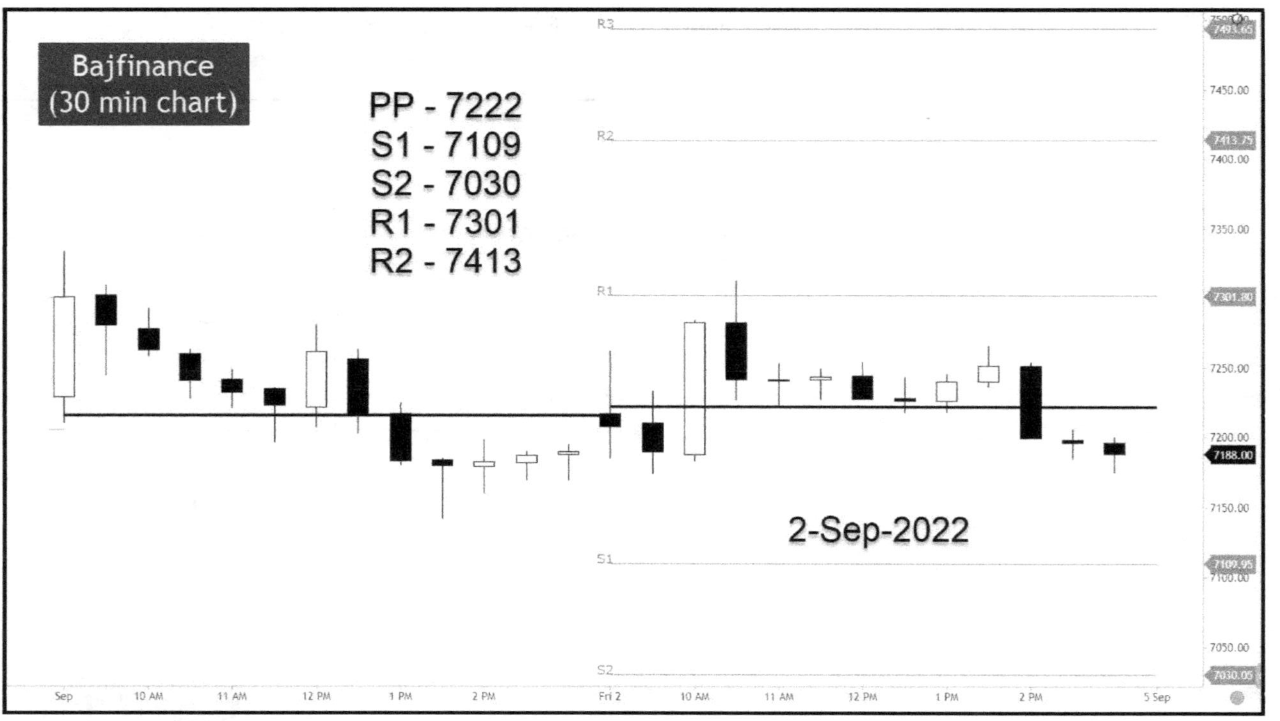

Image 6.15: Pivot points for Bajaj Finance 30-minute chart for 2 September 2022

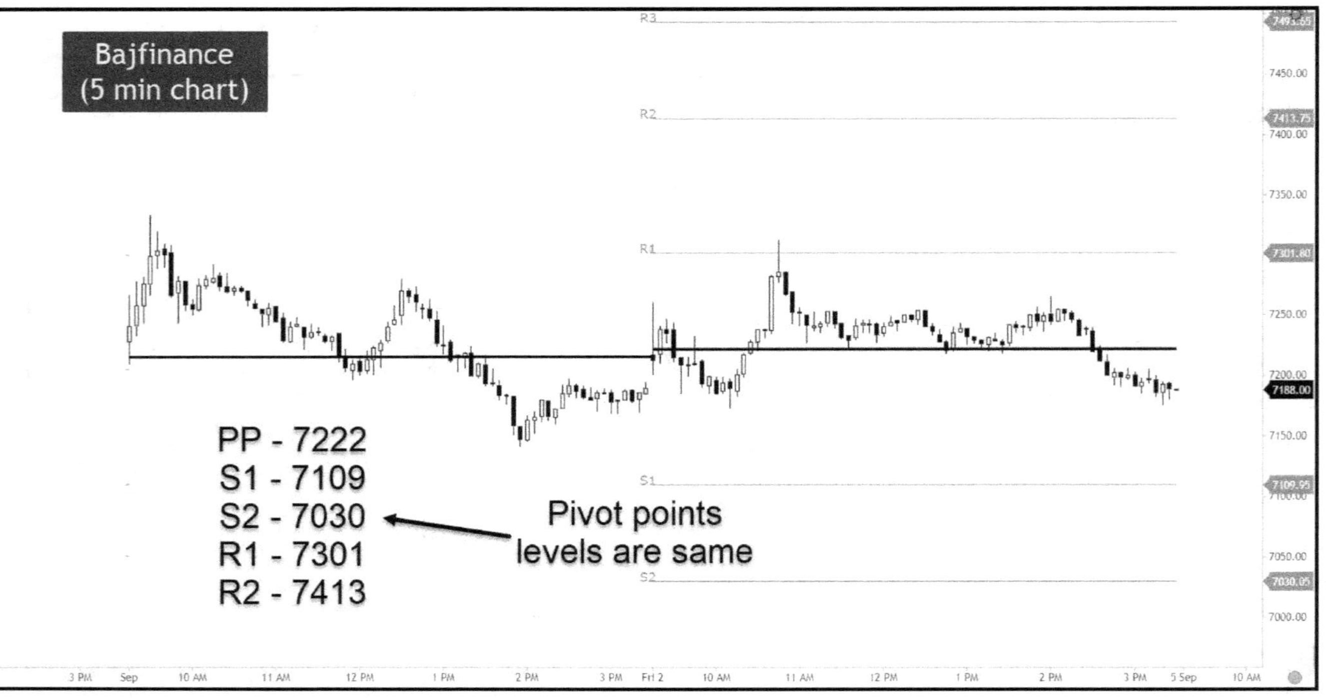

Image 6.16: Pivot points for Bajaj Finance 5-minute chart for 2 September 2022

These values are derived from the previous trading day. Even if you change the timeframe (in a live intraday market), it remains the same.

Image 6.16 shows the 5-minute chart for Bajaj Finance. As you can see, the pivot levels did not change.

2) If the price opens near PP, then S1 and R1 act as strong support and resistance

In image 6.17, the price opened near PP. It indicates the neutral behavior of the market. R1 and S1 act as resistance and support in highly probable cases in such situations. In this case, R1 acted as resistance, and the price stayed below R1 for most of the day.

3) If the price opens or breaks beyond R1 (open action), then the price moves in the upward direction

If the price opens and sustains above R1 or breaks above R1 in the open action, then there is a high probability of the price closing on the upside.

In image 6.18, the price broke above R1 in the first 5 minutes after the market opened. It indicates bulls are strong, so, the price closed near R3 on the same day.

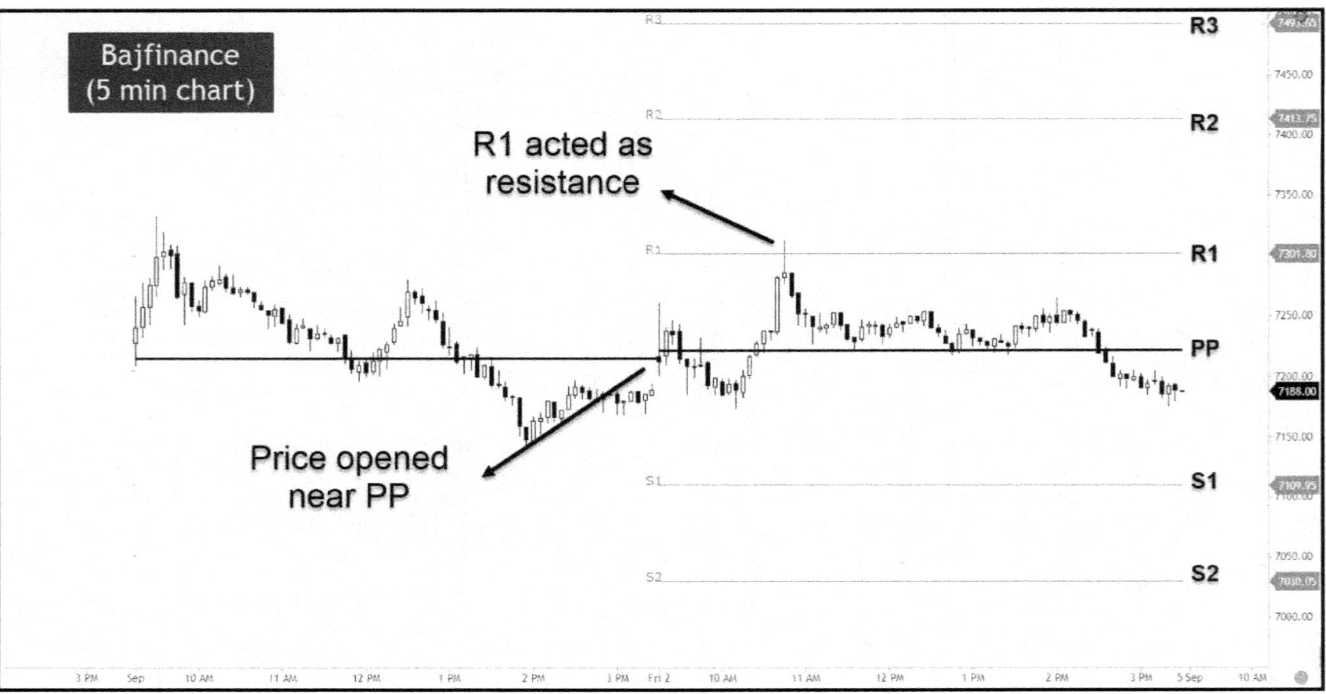

Image 6.17: R1 acted as resistance

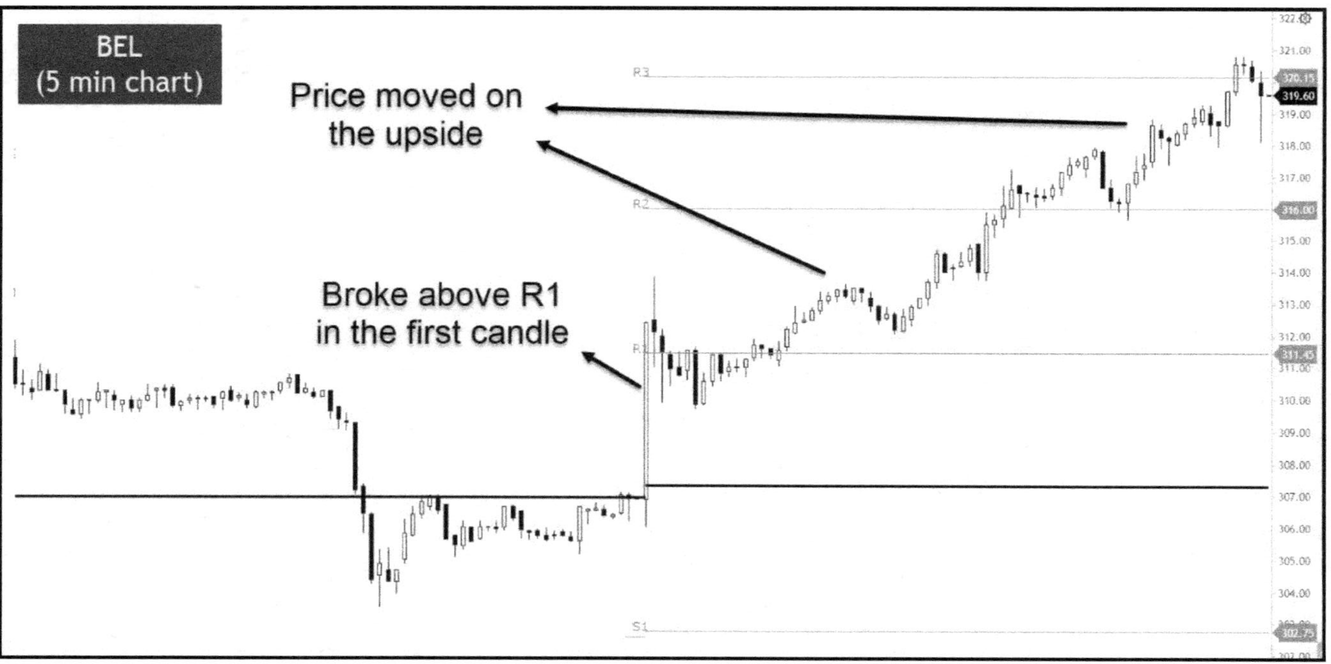

Image 6.18: Price moves above R1

4) If the price opens or breaks below **S1** (open action), then the price moves in the downward direction

If the price opens and sustains below S1 or breaks below S1 in the open action, then there is a high probability of the price closing on the downside.

In image 6.19, the price opens and sustains below S1 in the first 5 minutes after the market opens. It indicates bears are strong, and therefore it is traded downside for the rest of the day.

It is important to remember that pivot points are only as good as the underlying data used to calculate them. For this reason, it is vital to use accurate data when constructing pivot point charts.

Additionally, it is essential to keep in mind that the market does not always move in a linear fashion. Pivot points may provide guidance, but they should not be relied upon blindly. As with all technical indicators, they should be used in conjunction with other forms of analysis.

Limitations

Pivot points are a popular tool used by technical traders to determine potential support and resistance levels in the market. However, they have several limitations that make them difficult to use as a stand-alone trading strategy.

Pivot points are based solely on past data and do not take into account overnight market sentiment.

Pivot points should never be used as an entry or exit strategy on their own. They can offer a valuable guide to potential support and resistance levels. Still, traders should look for confirmation of that price level before entering or exiting the market. Relying solely on pivot points as an entry or exit strategy will likely lead to losses over time.

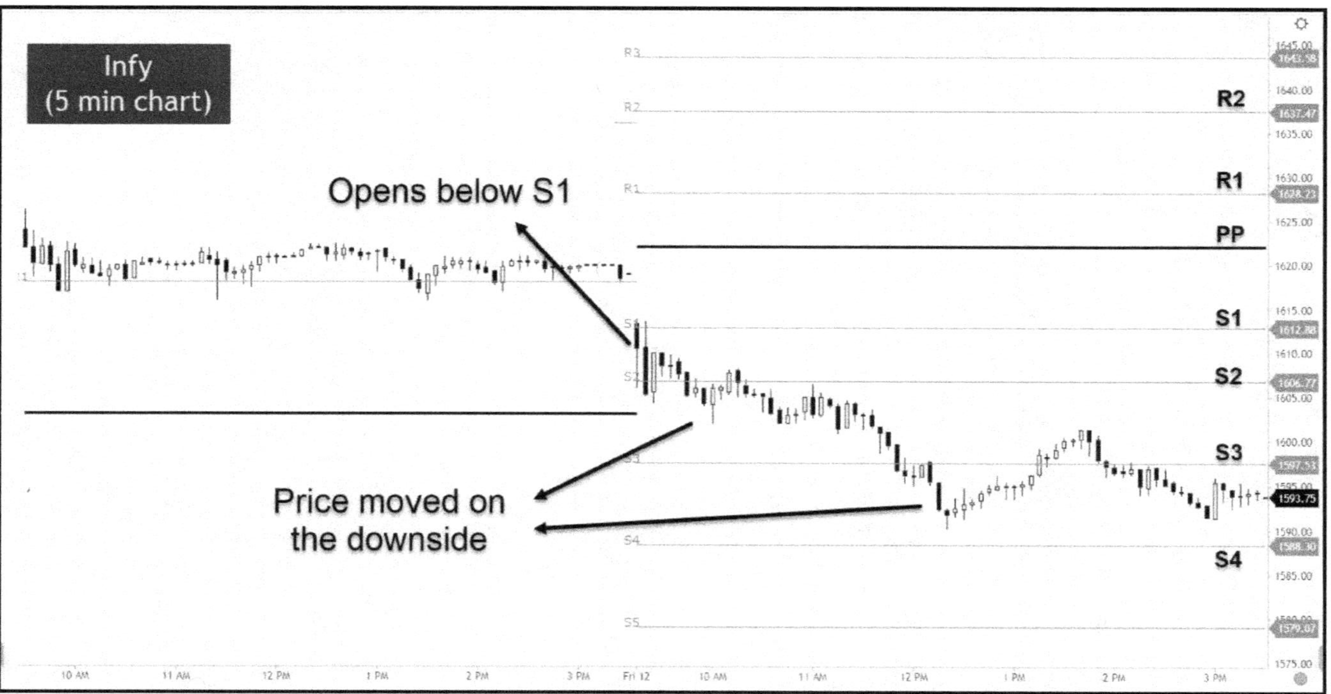

Image 6.19: Price moves above S1

There are also certain limitations associated with how traders calculate pivot points. Different formulae can be used to calculate pivot points, so it is crucial to understand which formula is used and if it applies to the current market environment.

5. CENTRAL PIVOT RANGE (CPR)

Central Pivot Range (CPR) indicator is similar to pivot points that are used to measure the range of price movement over a particular period. However, along with support (S1, S2, S3) and resistance (R1, R2, R3) lines, CPR consists of two additional lines below and above PP (Top central pivot point (TC) and Bottom central pivot point (BC) to form a pivot range.

CPR is generally used as a way to identify potential support and resistance levels, as well as to gauge the strength of trends.

Pivot Point = (High + Low + Close) / 3
Top Central Pivot Point (TC) = (Pivot − BC) + Pivot
Bottom Central Pivot Point (BC) = (High + Low) / 2

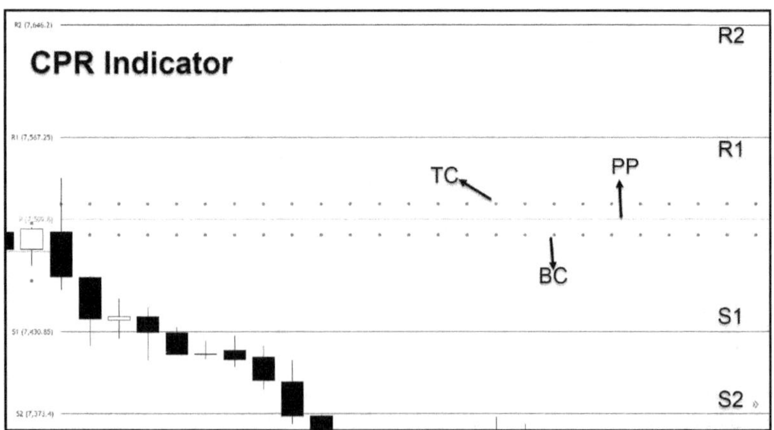

Image 6.20: CPR indicator

Below are some interesting characteristics of the CPR indicator in a daily timeframe.

1) High gap between **CPR** lines indicates a sideways market

If the gap between CPR lines is high (compared to the earlier few days), then there is a high probability of a sideways move on that particular trading day.

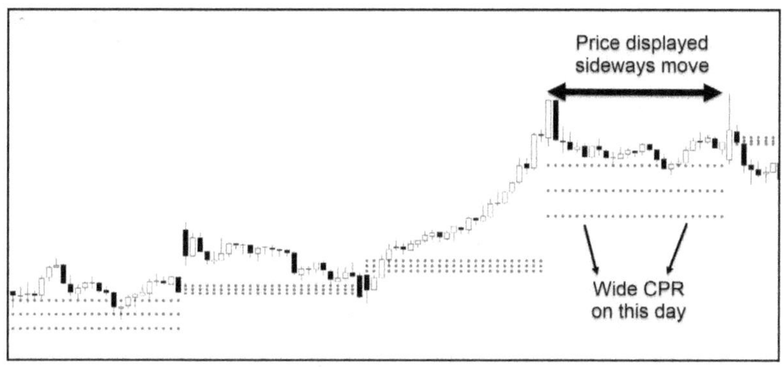

Image 6.21: Wide CPR results in sideways move

Image 6.21 showed wide CPR. On the same trading day, the price displayed a complete sideways move for the complete trading day.

2) Small gap between **CPR** lines indicates a trending market

If the gap between CPR lines is very narrow (compared to the earlier few days), then there is a high probability of a trending move on that particular trading day.

Image 6.22 showed a narrow CPR. On the same trading day, the price displayed a trending move (downside) for the rest of the day.

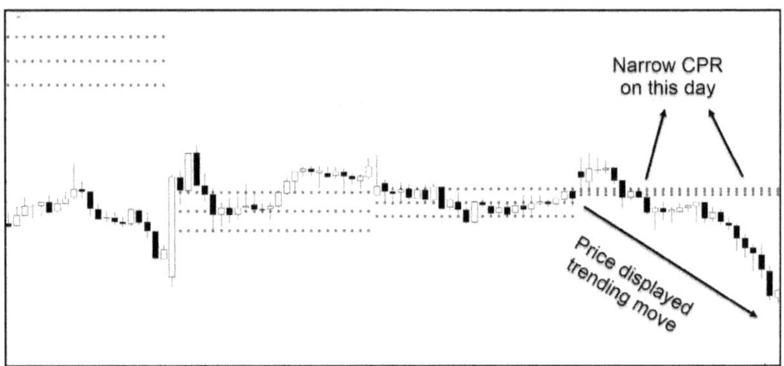

Image 6.22: Narrow CPR results in trending move

3) If the price opens and sustains above CPR, then it is bullish

In image 6.23, the price opened and sustained above CPR on two successive trading days. This indicates 'bullish,' and the price closed upside on both days.

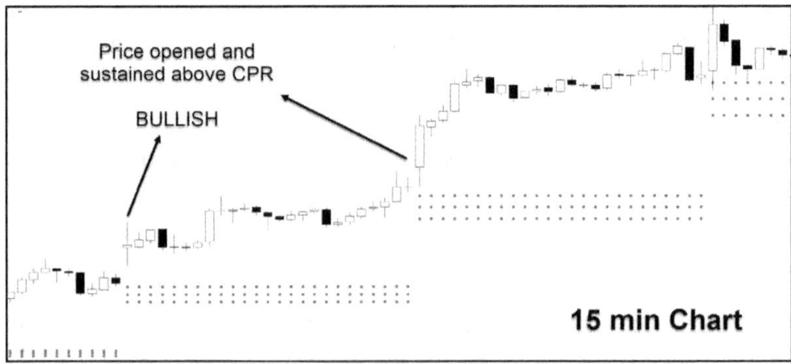

Image 6.23: If price opens above CPR, then it is bullish

4) If the price opens and sustains below CPR, then it is bearish

In image 6.24, the price opened and sustained below CPR on two successive trading days. This indicates a bearish trend, and the price closed downside on both days.

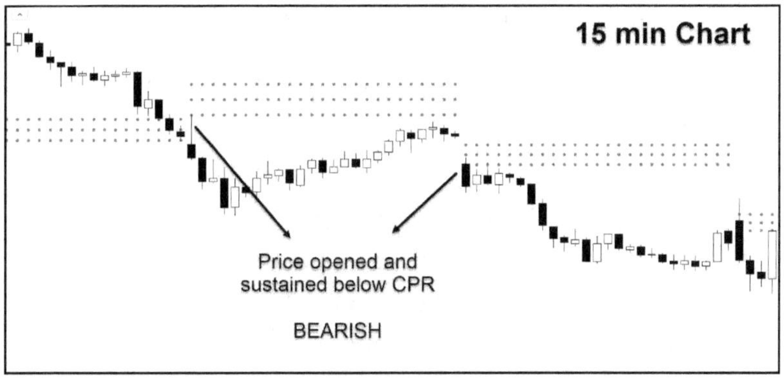

Image 6.24: Price opened below CPR is bearish

Overall, the CPR indicator is a helpful tool for technical analysis that can be used to measure the range of price movement, identify potential support and resistance levels, and gauge the strength of trends. When used in conjunction with other technical indicators, it can also help confirm trading signals.

Limitations CPR is similar to pivot points. Hence, some of the drawbacks of pivot points also occur for CPR.

1. CPR values are based solely on past data and do not consider overnight market sentiment.
2. Pivot points in CPR should never be used as an entry or exit strategy on their own. Traders should look for confirmation

of that price level before entering or exiting the market. Relying solely on pivot points or CPR as an entry or exit strategy will likely lead to losses over time.

3. Beginners might get confused about identifying wide CPR and narrow CPR. They need to practice for some time to understand this.

Which Indicator Is the Best?

As the name suggests, indicators provide only indications and are not 100% accurate.

All indicators have unique characteristics in different market conditions. An intelligent trader will pick a couple of indicators and study their behavior in different market conditions (uptrend, downtrend, sideways, volatile, etc.). Then he follows them religiously in the live market conditions without generating any doubt.

7

What Support and Resistance Can Teach Us About Big Players' Activity

When it comes to trading, the concepts of 'support' and 'resistance' are absolutely essential. If you don't understand these two terms, then you are less likely to see some profits in trading.

So, what are support and resistance? In a nutshell, support is the level at which traders are willing to buy an asset, while resistance is the level at which they are eager to sell it.

It's important to remember that these levels are not set in stone—they can change over time. However, they provide an excellent general guide on where prices are likely to find some sort of floor or ceiling.

Let's take a look at an example:

If you look at image 7.1, there is a strong level of support around the 200 level. This means that whenever the stock price falls to 200, there is a good chance that strong buyers will step in and buy it, driving the price back toward the upside.

In simple words, 'support' is a price level at which buying is strong enough to absorb all the selling.

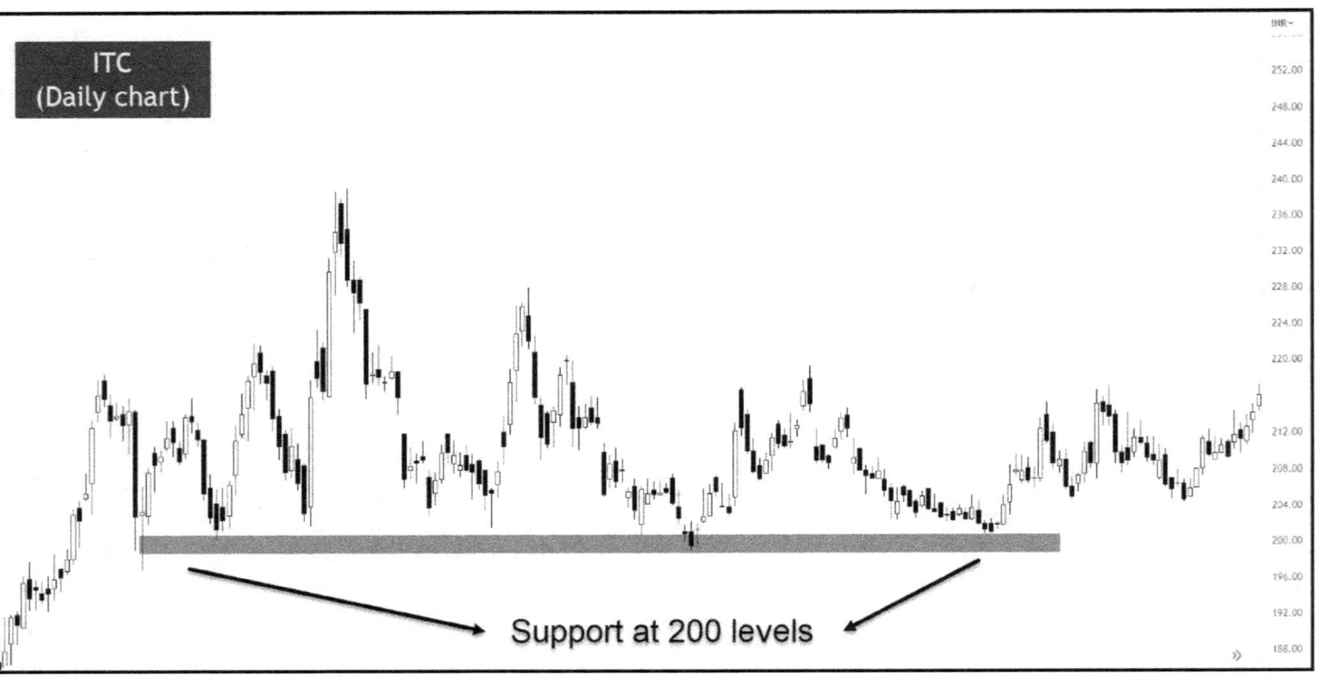

Image 7.1: Support at 200 in ITC

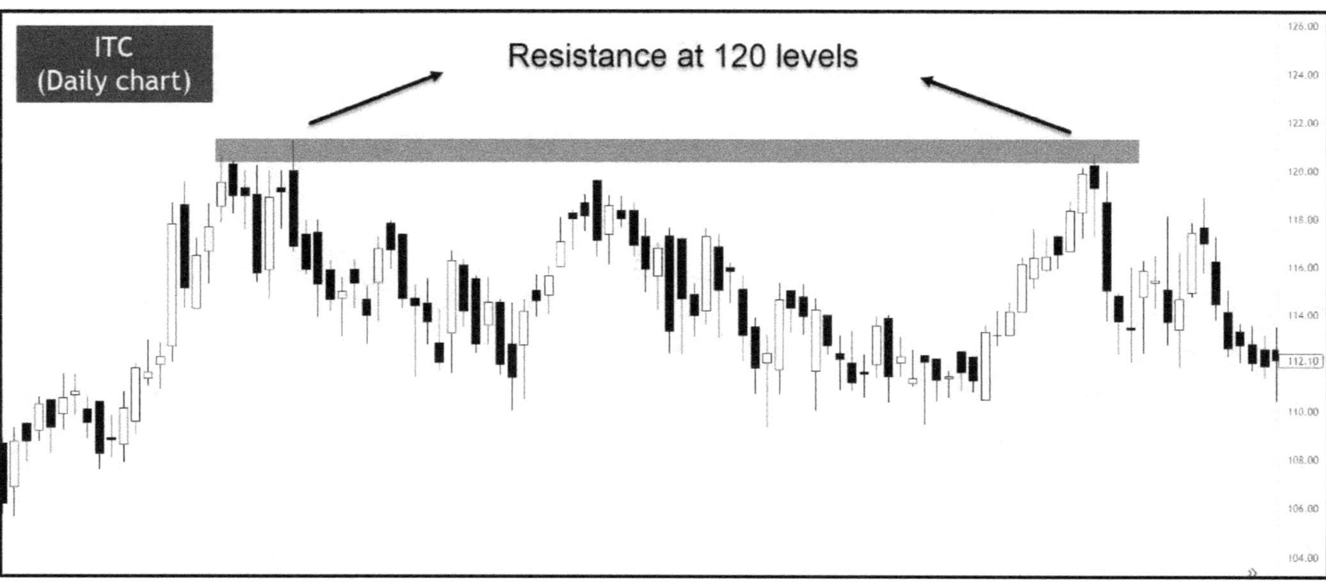

Image 7.2: Resistance at 120 in ITC

If you look at image 7.2, there is a strong level of resistance around 120 levels (before forming support at 200, as shown in 7.1). This means that whenever the stock price rises to 120, there is a good chance that strong sellers will step in and sell it, driving the price back toward the downside.

Simply put, 'resistance' is a price level at which selling is strong enough to absorb all the buying.

A support trend line is a straight line that connects two or more price points on a chart and is used to identify the market's overall direction.

The slope of the line indicates the rate of change in price, with a positive slope indicating an upward trend and a negative slope indicating a downward trend. These support and resistance lines can also occur with a slight slope.

Image 7.3 and 7.4 show support and resistance trend lines with a slope. Beginners should consider the points mentioned below while drawing support or resistance trend lines:

Image 7.3: Support trend line with a slope

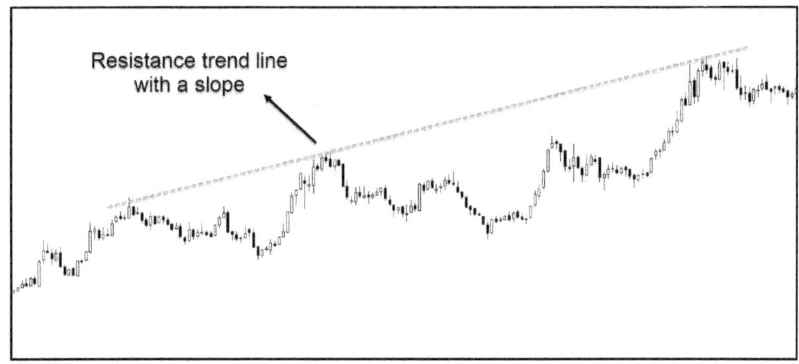

Image 7.4: Resistance trend line with a slope

1. Try to join a minimum of 3 peaks. The impact of the trend line will be higher with a higher number of peaks.

2. Due to price volatility, we may not be able to connect all the peaks with a simple line. In that case, you can use a small zone or band to draw the lines (as shown in image 7.1 and image 7.2).

3. The steep (angle) of the trend line is important. High steep indicates an unhealthy trend. The slope should always be less than 45 degrees.

4. Don't write too many trend lines in one chart. The idea of the trend line is to convey the trend and price movement in 1 to 2 lines.

5. Trend lines in higher timeframes take more importance compared to trend lines in a lower timeframe.

SUPPORT TURNING INTO RESISTANCE AND VICE-VERSA

A few years ago, 1 kg of regular rice cost around 20-30 rupees. Now the same rice costs approximately 60-80 rupees. There are many reasons for this — 1) inflation, 2) supply and demand, and 3) people's perception of supply and demand.

Let's assume a person worked in the rice business for many years. He sold rice for 25 rupees per kg for many years.

Now the price jumped to 35-40 rupees. He started selling rice at the new price.

After many days a close business associate comes and asks for the rice price. He informs him about the new price (35-40 rupees). But that person does not agree and starts a negotiation.

Let's assume he had accumulated vast quantities of rice at 10-15 rupees per kg from farmers.

Whatever the negotiation, he will not sell below 25 rupees.

Most people would do the same thing if they were in his position. Do you agree?

It is because he had made a lot of sales earlier at 25 rupees per kg. Hence, level 25 occupied an important role in his subconscious mind.

Similar logic applies to trading as well.

The level which was once resistance, after the breakout, acts as support.

Image 7.5 and 7.6 show classic examples of resistance turning to support. In Tata Motors chart, level 370 acted as resistance a few times in 2021. The price broke this level in October 2021, and later the same level acted as support in March, May, and July 2022. A similar pattern can be seen in the Canara Bank chart as well.

Image 7.5: Tata Motors weekly chart (resistance turning to support)

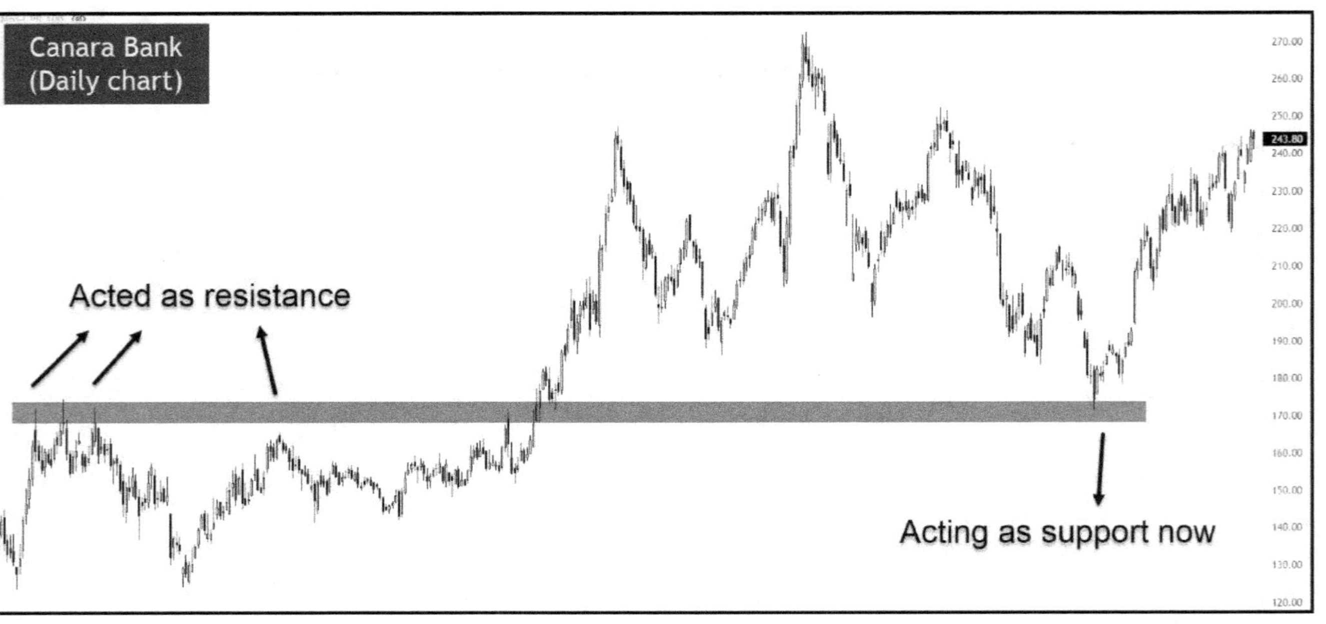

Image 7.6: Canara Bank daily chart (resistance turning to support)

Once again, images 7.7 and 7.8 are clear examples of how a price range that acted as support earlier can act as resistance in the later stages.

How to Use Support and Resistance in Trading?

Let's assume you want to excel in swing trading or positional trading (where the holding period varies from a few days to a few weeks).

Then you can look at the points below on a daily chart before opting for a trade:

1. Look for the strong trend, and your aim should be to take the trade only in the direction of the trend.
2. Ensure the price is giving a pullback near support levels or showing a breakout from the resistance levels.
3. You can opt for the long trade, keeping a stop-loss below the support or resistance level.
4. Exit some portion in the following crucial resistance level (if any), and carry the remaining with trail stop-loss.

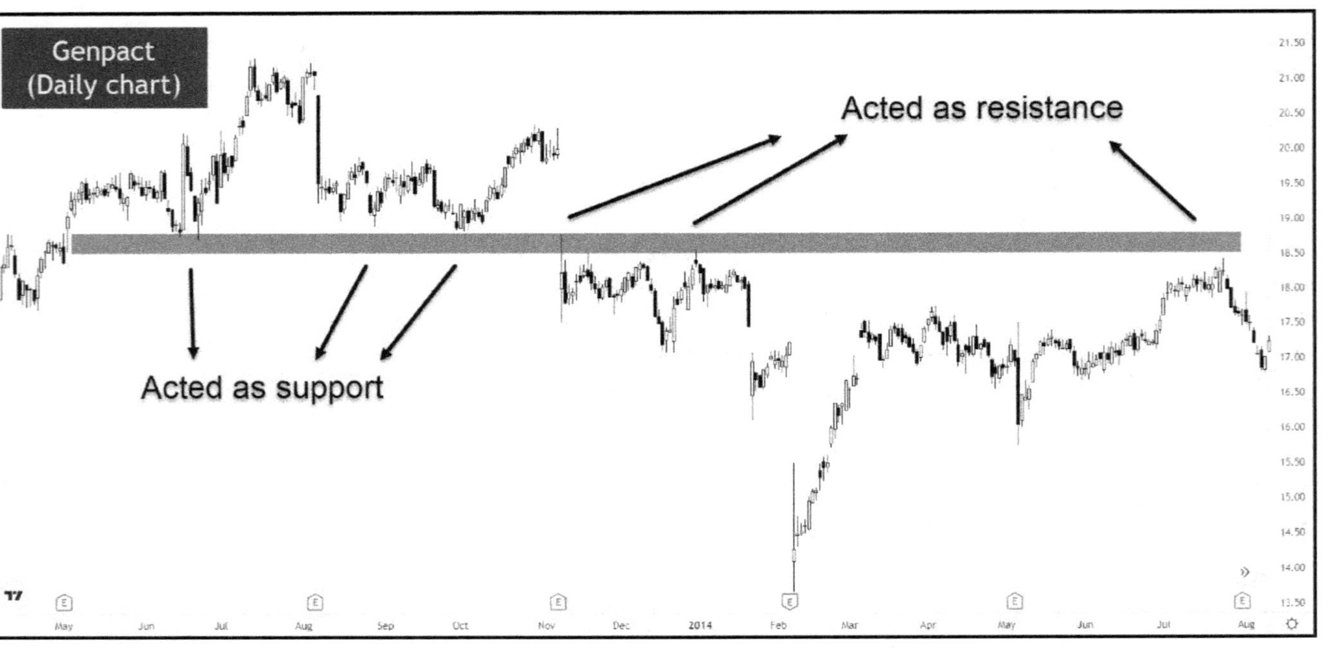

Image 7.7: Genpact daily chart (support turning to resistance)

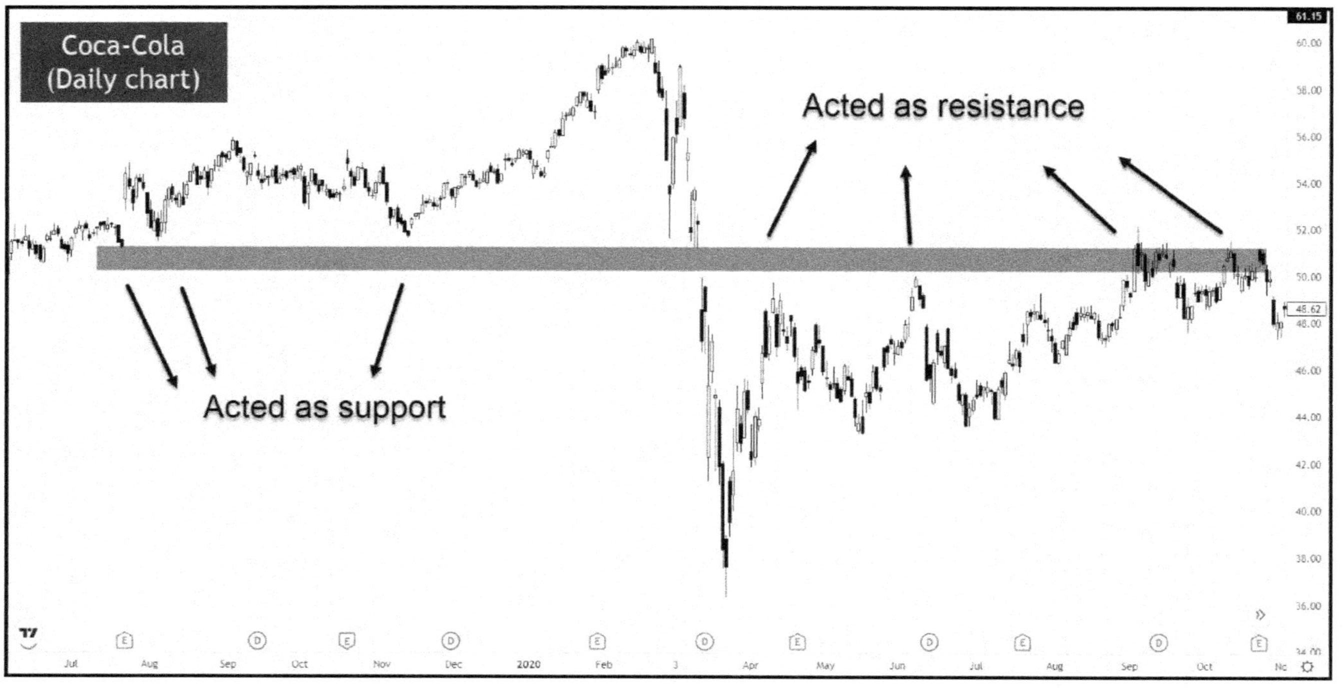

Image 7.8: Coca Cola daily chart (support turning to resistance)

Image 7.9 and 7.10 show examples of a long trade. In both cases, the original trend was up; the price displayed a clear breakout of the resistance trend line.

Traders can plan a long trade above the breakout candle, keeping a stop-loss below the low of the breakout candle. One can book a 50% position at 1:2 risk-reward and carry the remaining position with trailing stop-loss (TSL) below every swing low.

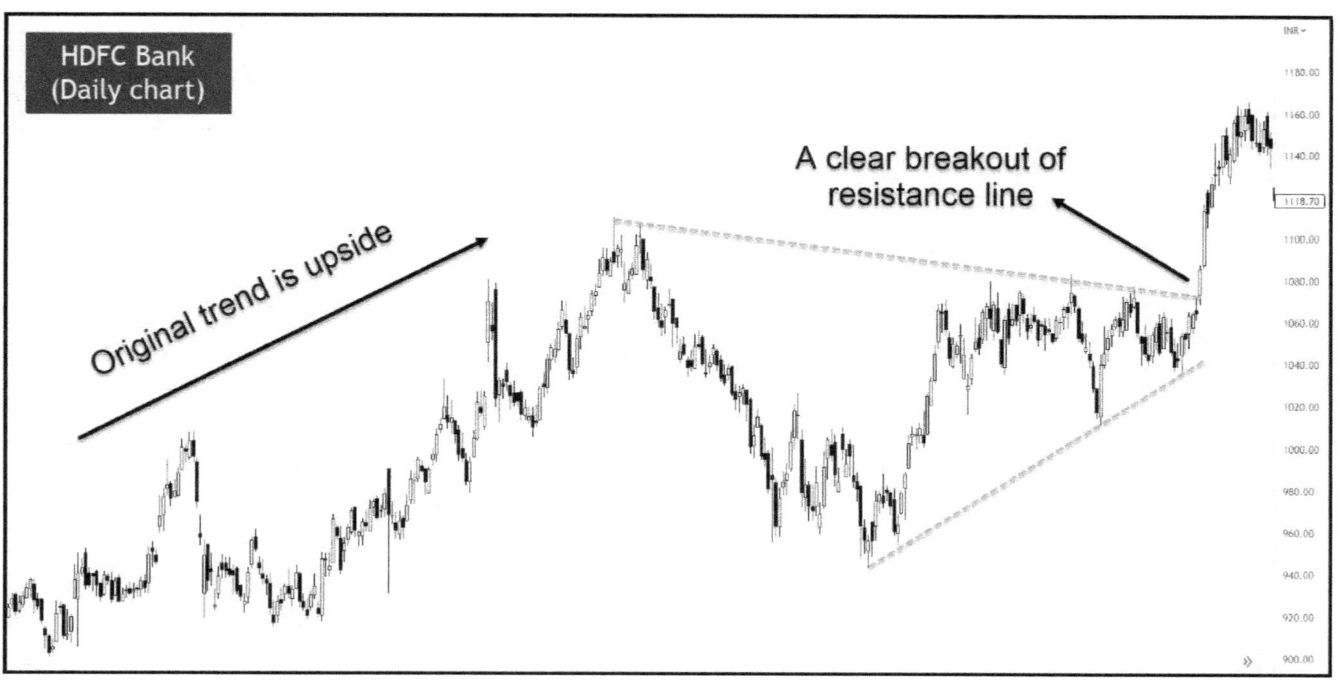

Image 7.9: Breakout entry in HDFC Bank

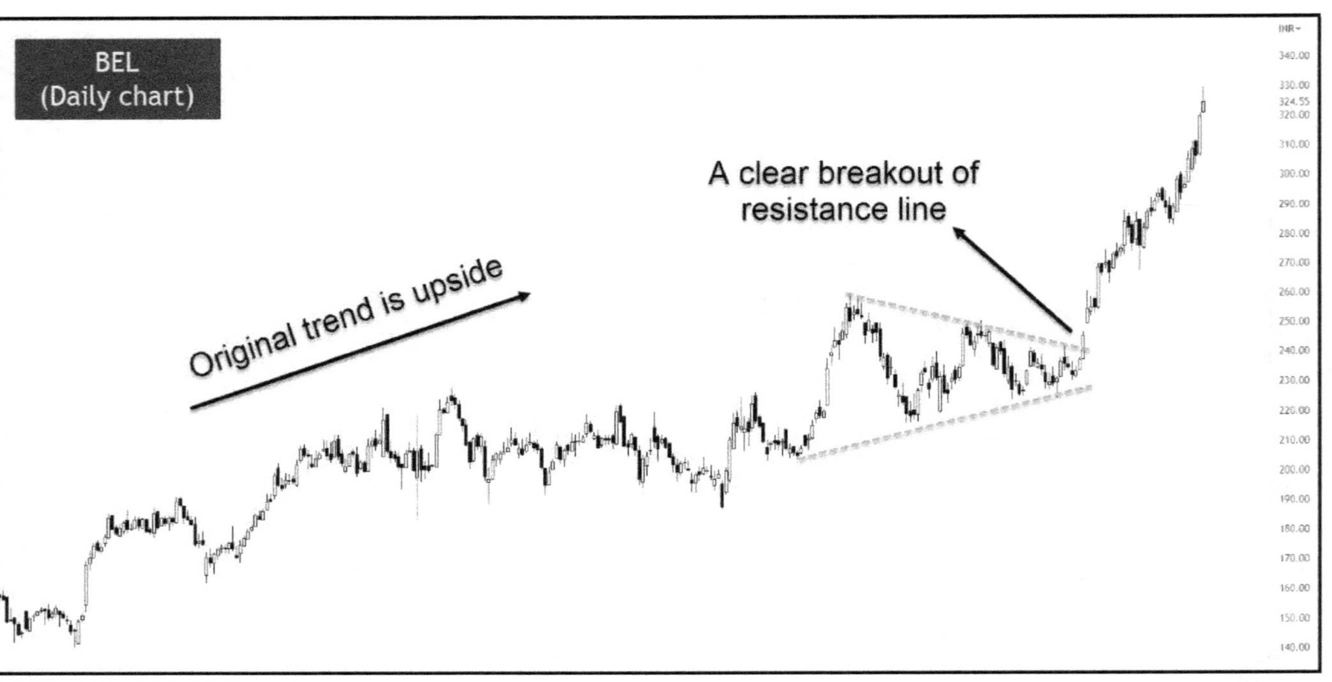

Image 7.10: Breakout entry in BEL

8

Moving Average and RSI Trading System

When developing a simple positional trading system, there are a few key things to keep in mind:

1. The system should have clearly defined entry, stop-loss, and exit rules.
2. The system should be able to adapt to different market conditions. In other words, it should be profitable in the long run.
3. The system should provide enough trade opportunities on most trading days.

One of the biggest mistakes traders make when developing their own systems is not defining entry, stop-loss, and exit rules.

Another mistake that many traders make is to develop a complicated trading system. A good trading system should be easy to use and understand. If a trader cannot understand how the system works, chances are they will not be successful in using it.

Please do your own research before using any of the systems mentioned in this book. Besides, back testing also brings conviction to your mind and helps to manage trades efficiently.

This system has two components–moving average and RSI.

System Rules:

Chart – Daily Chart

Moving Average – 5 EMA and 50 EMA

RSI – Default 14-Period

Entry (Long Trade) – When 5 EMA crosses above 50 EMA from the downside, and RSI crosses 60 within a difference of one trading day (either on the same day, one day before, or one day after).

Exit – When 5 EMA crosses below 50 EMA from the upside.

Position Size – Do not deploy more than 10% of your trading capital per trade. If you have Rs. 1,00,000, then buy shares worth Rs. 10,000.

Example 1: Reliance

Image 8.1 shows an example of trade under this system.

On 17 August 2021, 5 MA traded above 50 MA, and RSI closed above 60 on the previous trading day.

So, entry comes during the next day's open candle (that is, on 18 August 2021) at 2170.

We need to hold the trade until 5 MA stays above 50 MA. Therefore, exited trade on 9 November 2021 at 2514 levels.

It made a profit of **16%** in less than 3 months.

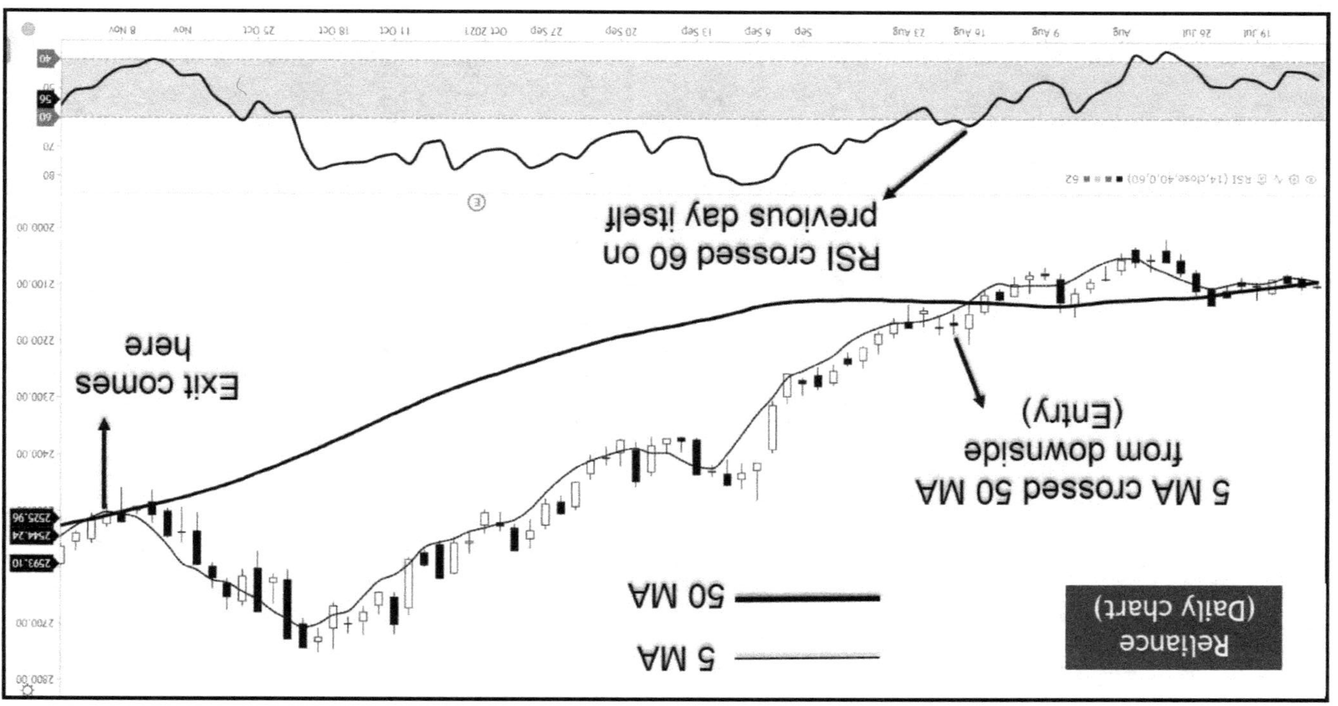

Image 8.1: MA and RSI position system in Reliance

Example 2: HDFC Bank

Image 8.2 shows another example of trade under this system.

On 5 October 2020, 5 MA traded above 50 MA, and RSI closed above 60 on the same trading day.

So, the entry happens during the next day's open candle (that is, on 6 October 2021) at 1132.

We need to hold the trade until 5 MA stays above 50 MA. Hence, exited trade on 1 February 2021 at 1422 levels.

Therefore, it made a profit of **25.6%** in less than 4 months.

Example 3: Twitter

Image 8.3 shows another example of a trade under this system.

On 1 February 2021, 5 MA traded above 50 MA, and RSI closed above 60 on the previous trading day.

Here, entry comes during the next day's open candle (that is, on 2 February 2021) at 52.7.

We need to hold the trade until 5 MA stays above 50 MA. In this case, we exited early on 29 March 2021 at 62.

So, it made a profit of **17.6%** in less than 2 months.

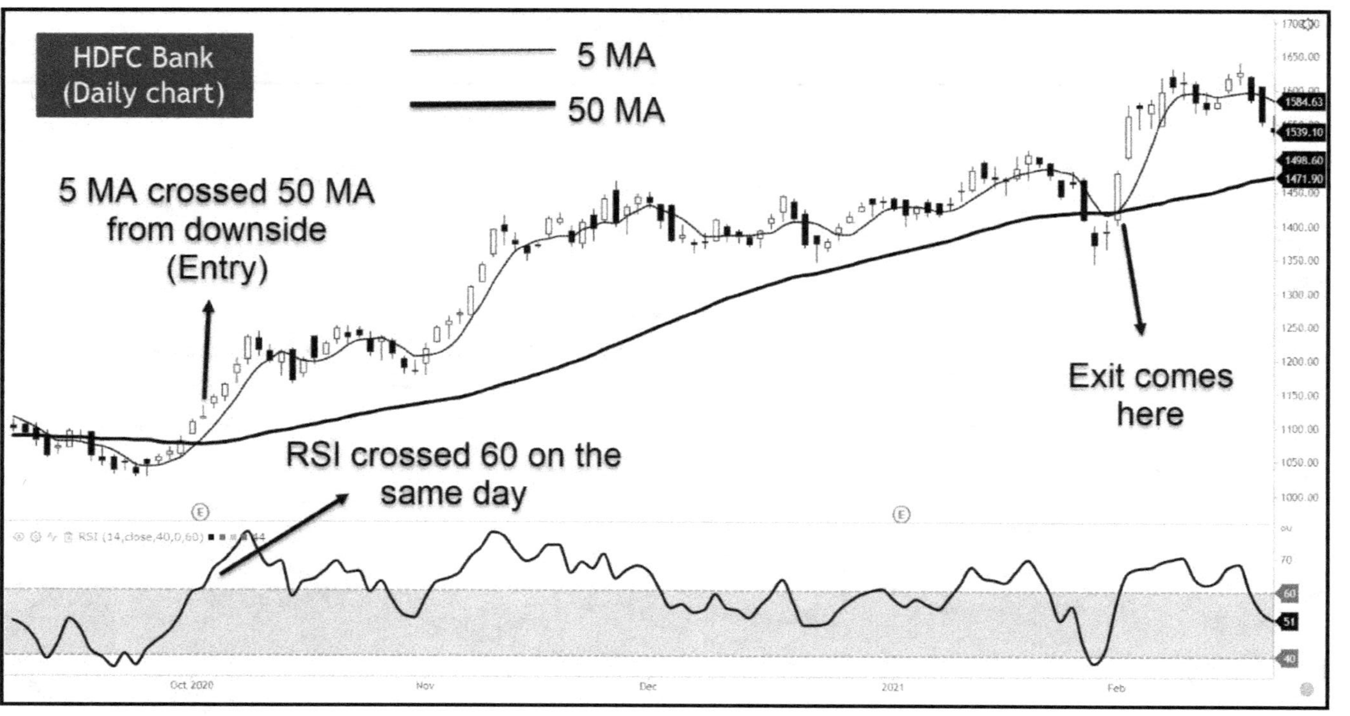

Image 8.2: Positional trade in HDFC Bank

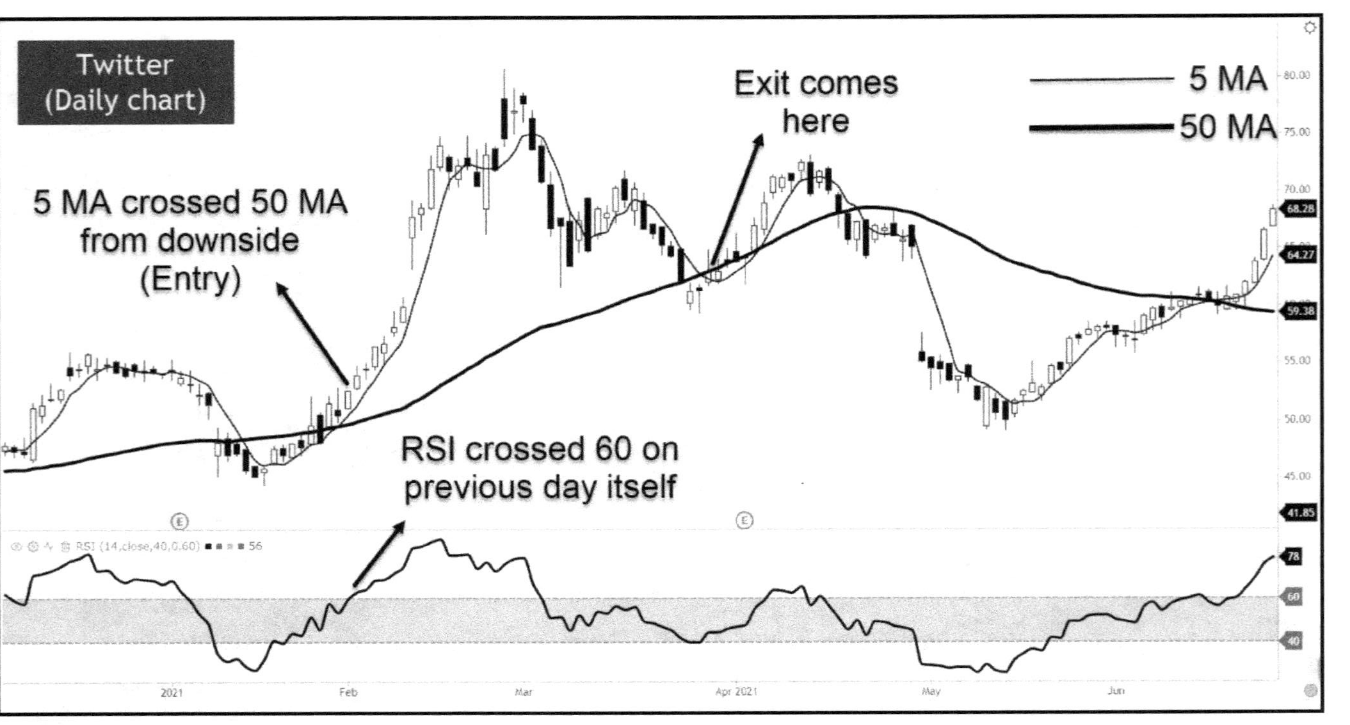

Image 8.3: Positional trade in Twitter

EXAMPLE 4: LOEWS CORPORATION

Image 8.4 shows another example of a trade under this system.

On 4 November 2020, 5 MA traded above 50 MA, and RSI closed above 60 on the previous trading day.

So, entry comes during the next day's open candle (that is, on 5 November 2020) at 36.3.

We need to hold the trade until 5 MA stays above 50 MA. In this case, exit came early on 15 June 2021 at 55.7.

It made a profit of **53.4%** in less than 7 months.

EXAMPLE 5: KELLOGG

When following this system, we should not break the rules. For example, skipping RSI > 60 rule is not a good idea.

If you look at image 8.5, 5 MA crossed above 50 MA a few times, but RSI is below 60, so we should not opt for this trade. This is how this system avoids unnecessary trades in the sideways market.

But in the end, the crossover happened again, and RSI was 60, and the price skyrocketed within a few days.

PRECAUTIONS

When following a positional trading system, there are a few key things to keep in mind to succeed.

First and foremost, verify the result of the system with historical data for 500-1000 charts. This will give you the confidence and conviction to follow the system in the long run.

Secondly, investing only 10% of your capital per trade is important. Even this system can fail sometimes, and if you risk more per trade, you might lose more capital.

Image 8.4: Positional trade in Loews Corporation

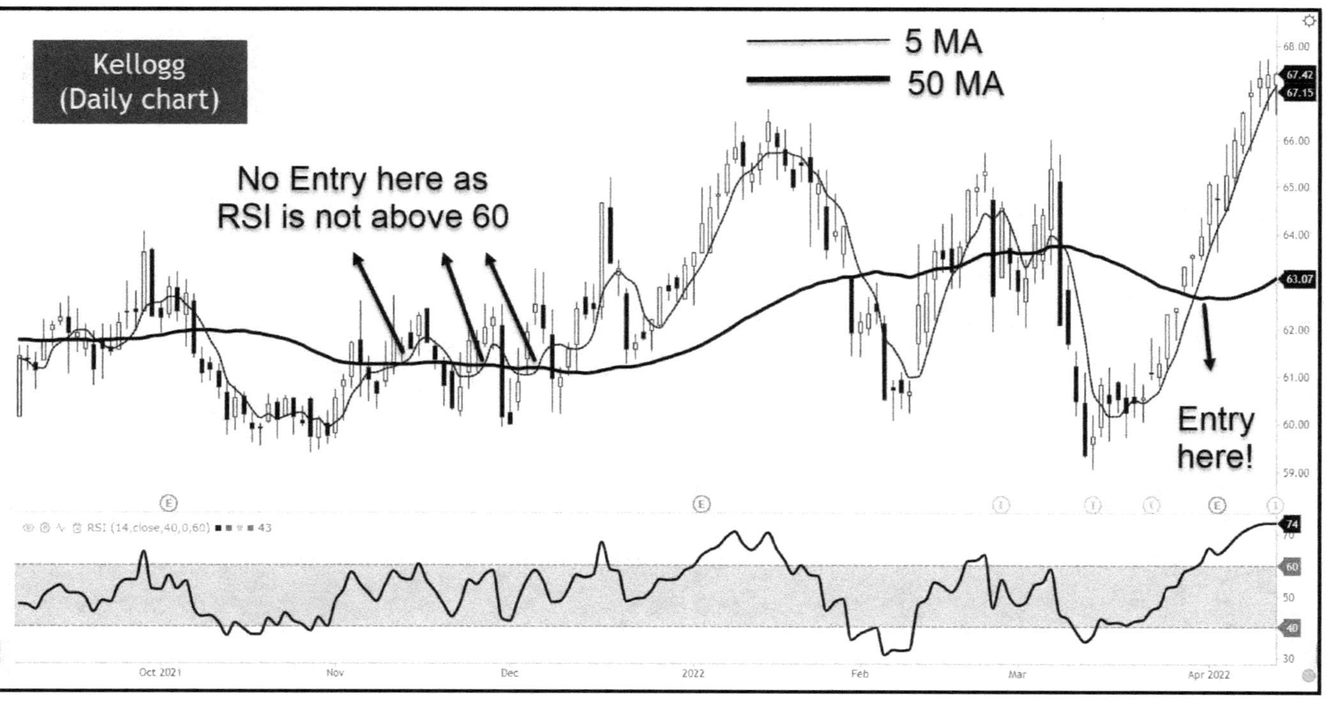

Image 8.5: Positional trade in Kellogg

Finally, it is also essential to be patient and let the trade play out. This is a system that aims to capture a big trend in the market. Profit from one trade can absorb the losses of 25 to 100 trades. Therefore, patience and persistent efforts are essential to achieve success using this system.

9

Things That Make You Love and Hate Chart Patterns

Chart patterns are one of the most essential tools that traders use to make decisions in financial markets. They are created by the movement of prices on a chart and can be used to predict price movements which occur in the future. Each pattern has its own unique characteristics and can provide traders with valuable information about the direction in which the market will move.

There are different chart patterns, but they can be broadly classified into two categories: reversal patterns and continuation patterns.

Reversal patterns occur when the price of an asset reverses direction after reaching a peak or trough. The most common reversal pattern is the head and shoulders pattern, which is considered a bearish reversal pattern.

Continuation patterns occur when the price of an asset continues in the same direction after a period of consolidation. The most common continuation pattern is the flag pattern, which is considered a bullish continuation pattern.

Chart patterns are not perfect, and should be used in conjunction with other technical indicators to make the most informed decisions possible. Nevertheless, they can be beneficial for any trader in financial markets.

Many chart patterns can be used in trading, but some of the most popular and reliable patterns include:

1. Head and shoulders
2. Double top and double bottom
3. Cup and handle
4. Flag
5. Symmetrical triangle

1. HEAD AND SHOULDERS

This reversal pattern typically forms after an extended uptrend and signals that the trend is about to reverse. The head and shoulders pattern is created when the price of an asset forms two higher highs followed by a lower high, typically in the form of a left shoulder, head, and right shoulder.

The head and shoulders pattern is considered to be a bearish reversal pattern, which means that it typically forms at the end of an uptrend and signals a potential change in direction from up to down. Image 9.1 shows how a head and shoulders appears in general.

Once the right shoulder forms and the neckline is broken, it is often used as a signal to enter a short position or to sell an existing long position.

Image 9.2 shows an example of a head and shoulders pattern in Nifty. It was in an uptrend before the formation of this pattern.

First, it formed a left shoulder, then a head (higher high), then another shoulder. The break of the neckline resulted in a fall.

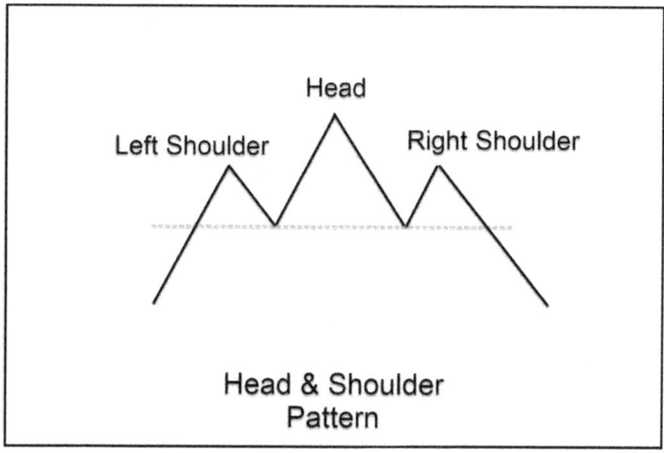

Image 9.1: Head and shoulders pattern

Sometimes these head and shoulders patterns also appear with a slight angle. Image 9.3 shows an angled head and shoulders pattern in Nifty.

The key to successfully trading head and shoulders patterns is to wait for the neckline to break before entering a position. This is because there is still a possibility that the price could continue higher if the pattern does not complete and the neckline is not breached.

The head and shoulders pattern can also be found in different forms, such as inverted head and shoulders (image 9.4), which is considered a bullish reversal pattern. Inverted head and shoulders patterns form when the price of an asset creates two lower lows followed by a higher low, typically in the form of a right shoulder, head, and left shoulder.

The critical difference between head and shoulders patterns and inverted head and shoulders patterns is that head and shoulders patterns are found at the end of uptrends, while inverted head and shoulders patterns are located at the end of downtrends.

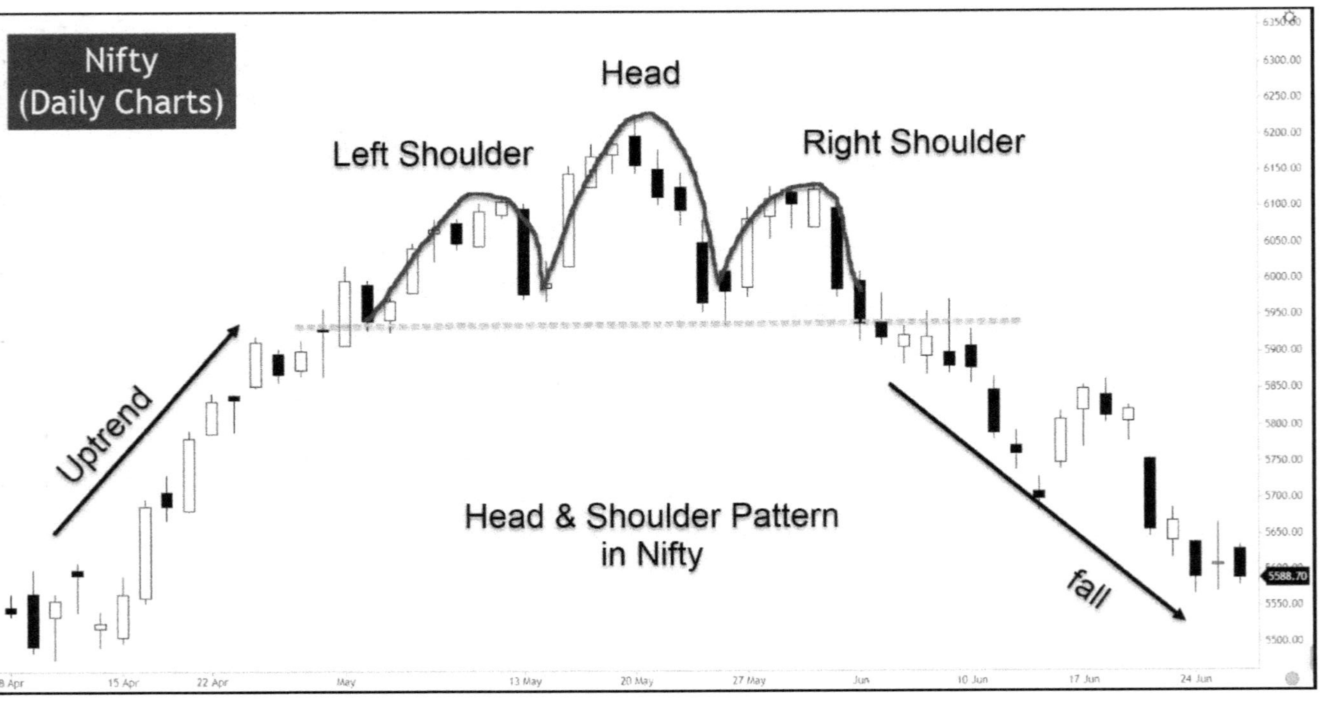

Image 9.2: Head and shoulders pattern in Nifty

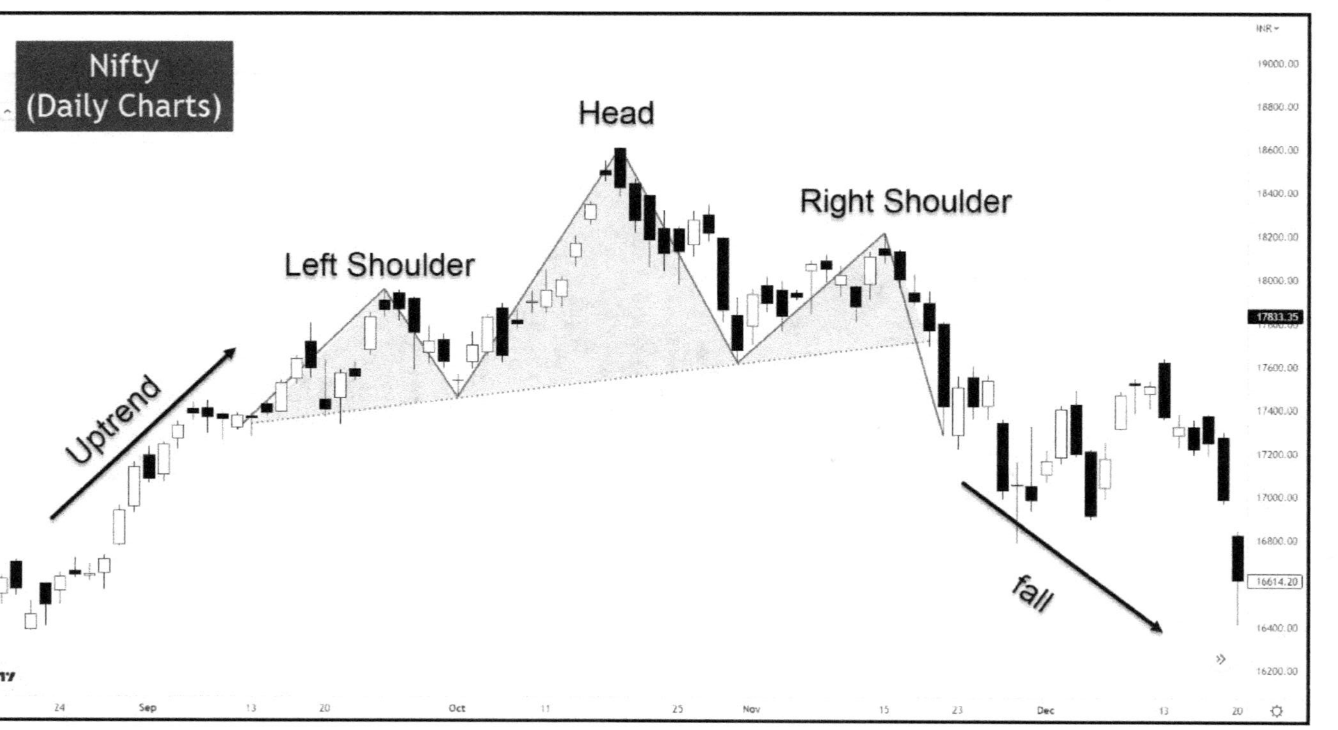

Image 9.3: Head and shoulders pattern (angled) in Nifty

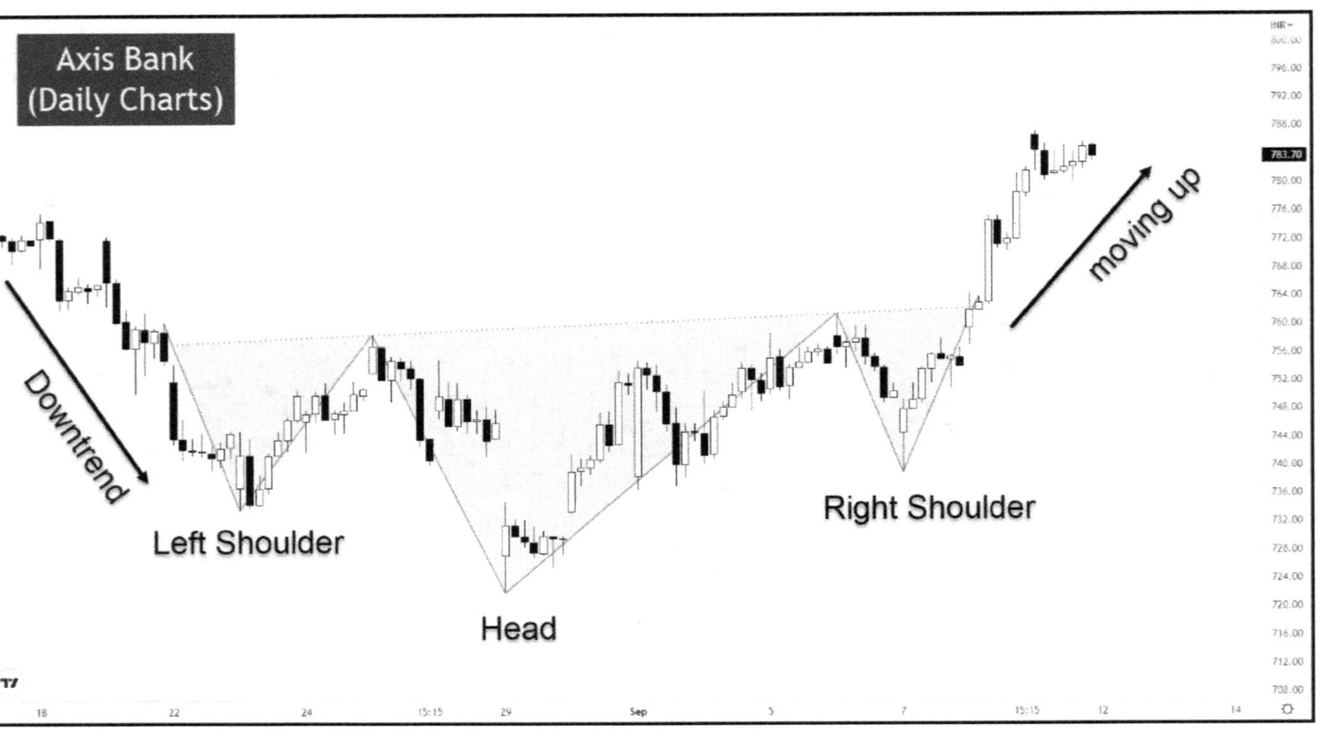

Image 9.4: Inverse head and shoulders pattern in Axis Bank

Trading head and shoulders patterns can be a profitable endeavor if done correctly. However, it is essential to remember that no technical analysis tool is 100% accurate; proper money management rules are always better for each trade.

2. Double Top and Double Bottom

These are reversal patterns that can form after an extended uptrend or downtrend.

Two consecutive peak prices create a double top. In comparison, a double bottom is formed by two successive trough prices. These patterns signal that the current trend is about to reverse.

Image 9.5 shows how a double top appears in general. A double top is a bearish reversal pattern that forms after an asset reaches a peak and retraces, only to reach the same peak a second time before dropping. The formation of a double top indicates that the sellers are gaining control and that the asset is likely to continue falling.

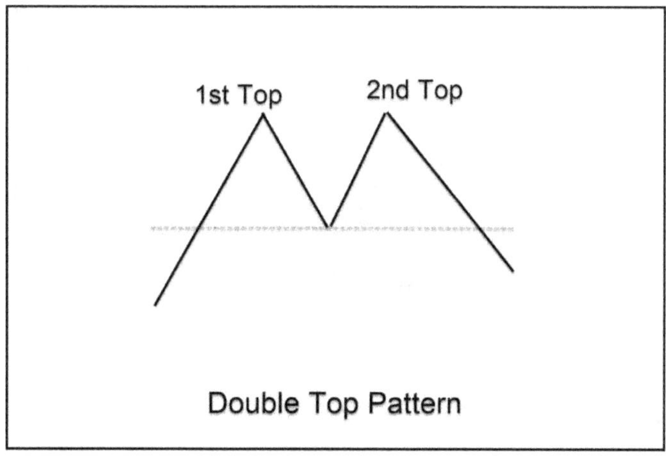

Image 9.5: Double top pattern

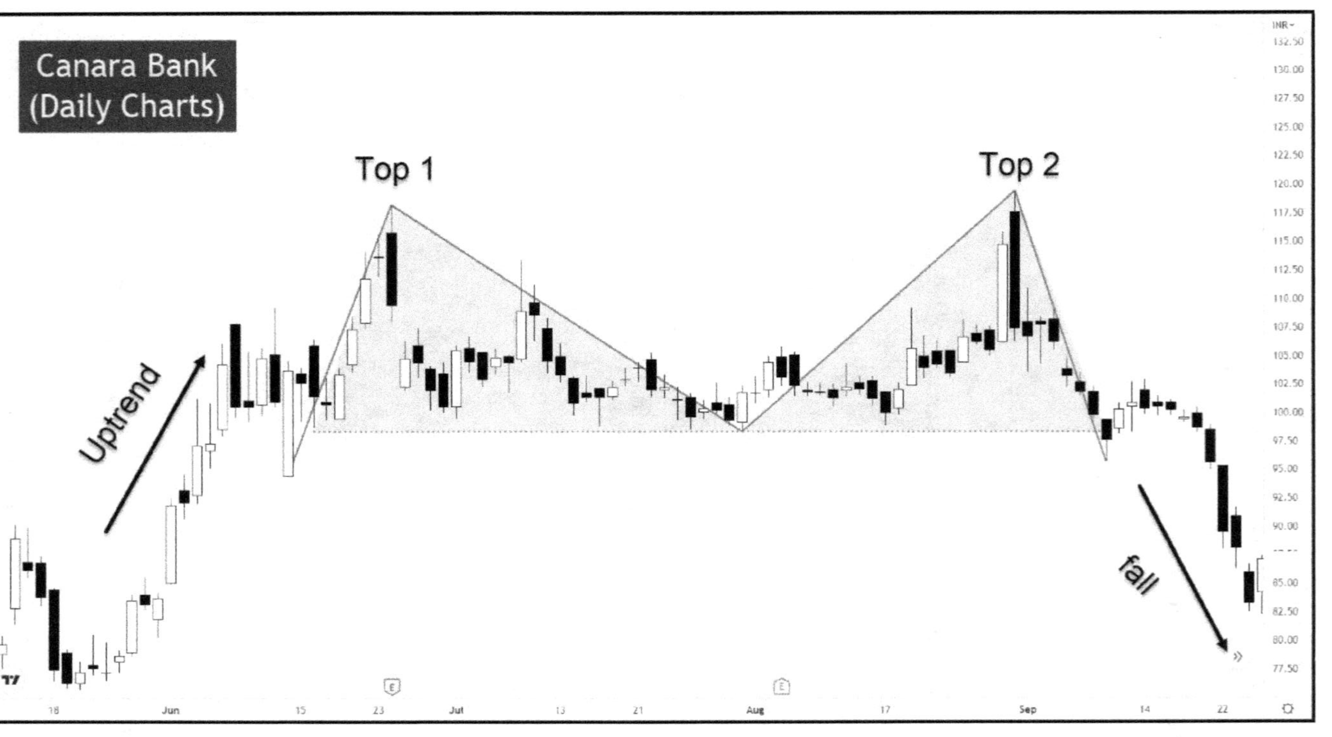

Image 9.6: Double top pattern in Canara Bank

The first step to identify a double top is to look for an asset that has been in an uptrend.

Once you have found a stock in an uptrend, you will want to monitor it for a potential double top.

A double top typically forms after the asset reaches a new high and returns to support. The key is that the retracement should not move below the previous low. If it does, this is likely not a double top.

Once the stock has retraced back to support, it will typically attempt to rally back to the previous high. This is where you will want to look for the formation of the double top.

The double top is formed when the asset fails to break above the previous high and instead forms a second peak. After forming the second peak, the asset will then continue falling as sellers start to take control.

The neckline of a double top is created by connecting the lows of the retracement between the two peaks.

This line acts as support and resistance and can be used to help confirm whether or not a double top has formed.

A break below the neckline would signal that a valid double top has formed, and that the asset is likely to continue falling.

Image 9.6 shows an example of a double top pattern in the Canara Bank chart. It made two same tops, and when the price broke the neckline, it fell quickly.

The double bottom pattern is similar to the double top pattern but on the opposite side (image 9.7). The key to finding this pattern is to look for two distinct lows that are roughly equal in price. The second low should also be followed by a bullish reversal candlestick or bar.

This pattern forms when there is a sharp sell-off followed by a period of consolidation. Once the market finds support at first low, it will usually rally back toward the previous highs.

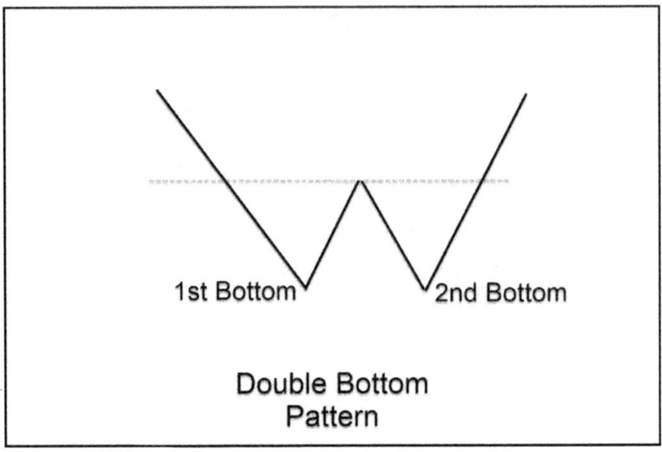

Image 9.7: Double bottom pattern

However, most of the time, the market will struggle to break through this resistance and eventually sell off again. This second sell-off will create the second low, where traders can look to enter long positions.

Image 9.8 shows an example of a double bottom pattern in Ebay Inc. The double-bottom pattern can provide traders with an excellent opportunity to enter long positions.

However, it is important to wait for confirmation before entering any trade. One way to confirm the double bottom pattern is to wait for a breakout above the previous high. This breakout can be used as an entry point into a long trade.

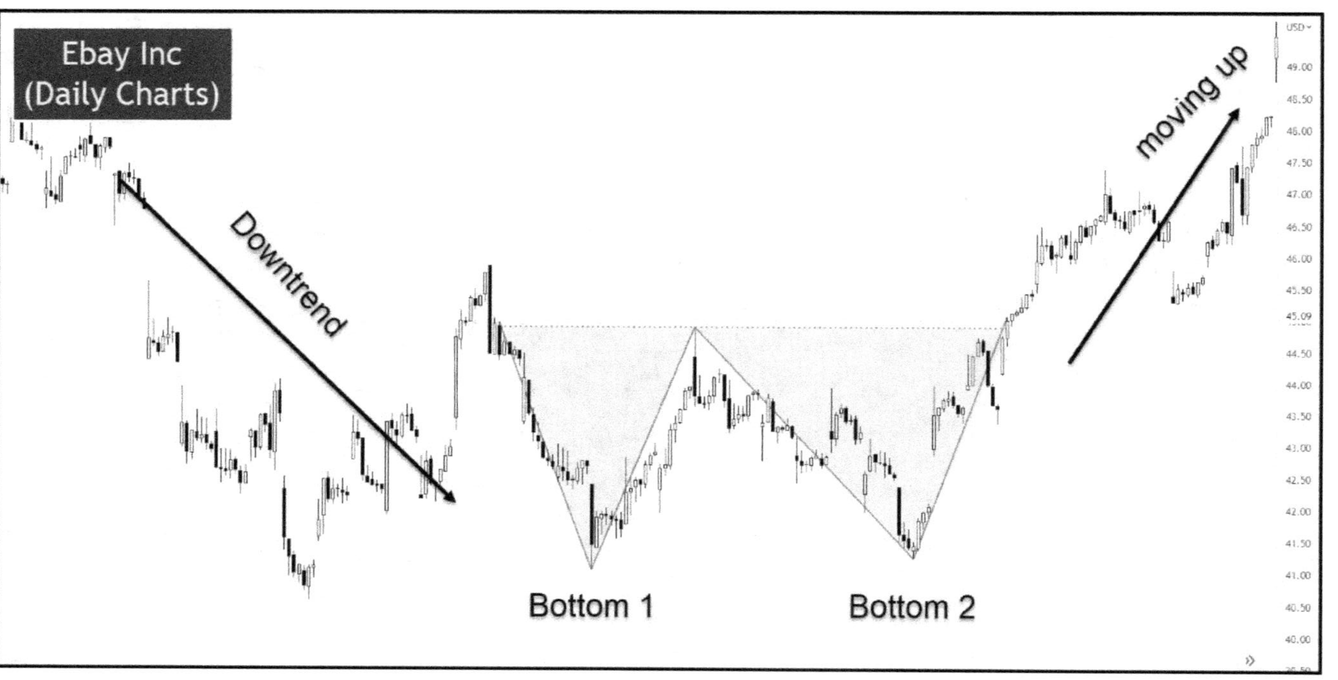

Image 9.8: Double bottom pattern in Ebay Inc.

3. Cup and Handle

The cup and handle pattern is a continuation chart pattern that marks a consolidation period followed by a breakout.

The pattern is created by a 'V' shaped price move, with the left side of the 'V' representing the consolidation period and the right side of the 'V' representing the breakout.

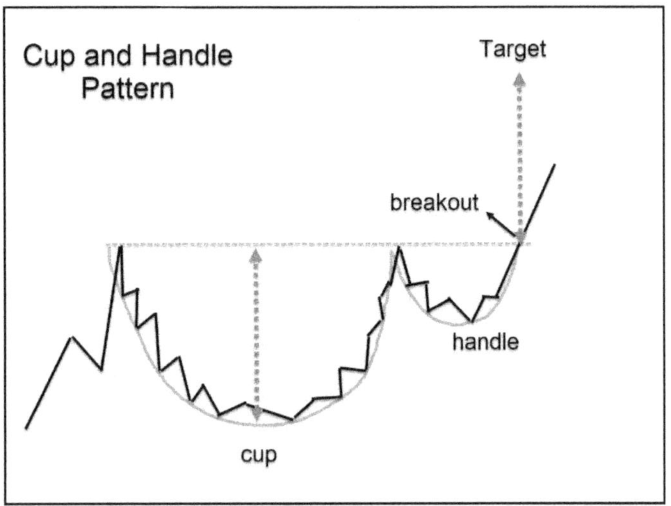

Image 9.9: Cup and handle pattern

The cup and handle pattern is considered a bullish continuation pattern. We can use it to identify entry points for long positions.

The key features of the cup and handle pattern are as follows:

1. There is a clear trend in place before the pattern forms.
2. The consolidation period marks a retracement in price against the prevailing trend.
3. The handle forms as the price consolidates within a tight range.
4. The handle is typically short-lived and marks a final period of consolidation before the breakout.

5. The breakout occurs to the upside, confirming the continuation of the underlying trend. Traders can target the height of the cup as their target on the upside.

Image 9.10 and 9.11 show examples of a cup and handle pattern in Adani Ports and Reliance stocks respectively. In both cases, the prior trend was up; the consolidation period is shown as a cup, and tight consolidation is shown as a handle. Once the price breaks the neckline, the price moves on the upside. Traders can target the height of the cup as their target on the upside once the price breaks the neckline.

The cup and handle pattern is a continuation chart pattern that can be used to identify potential entry points for long positions in an uptrending market.

The key features of the pattern are a clear trend, a consolidation period, a handle, and a breakout. The cup and handle pattern can be used with indicators such as the average directional moving index (ADX) to confirm the breakout because it represents the trend's strength. Any ADX value above 20-25 indicates a strong trend is in place.

4. Flag

The flag pattern is considered to be a continuation pattern, which typically occurs during an ongoing trend and signals that the trend will continue once the pattern completes.

There are two types of flag patterns–bull flag and bear flag.

A bull flag is created when the price action of stock forms a parallelogram shape after a sharp move higher or lower.

A bear flag is created when the price action of stock forms a parallelogram shape after a sharp fall.

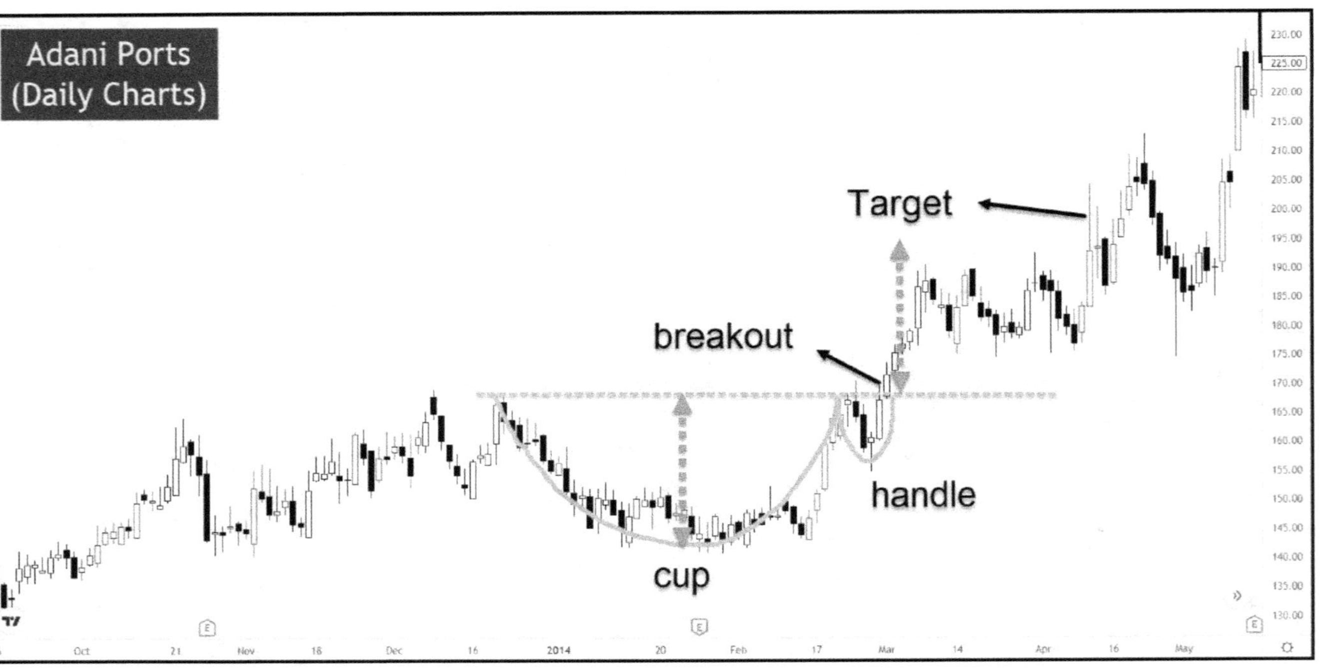

Image 9.10: Cup and handle pattern in Adani Ports

Image 9.11: Cup and handle pattern in Reliance

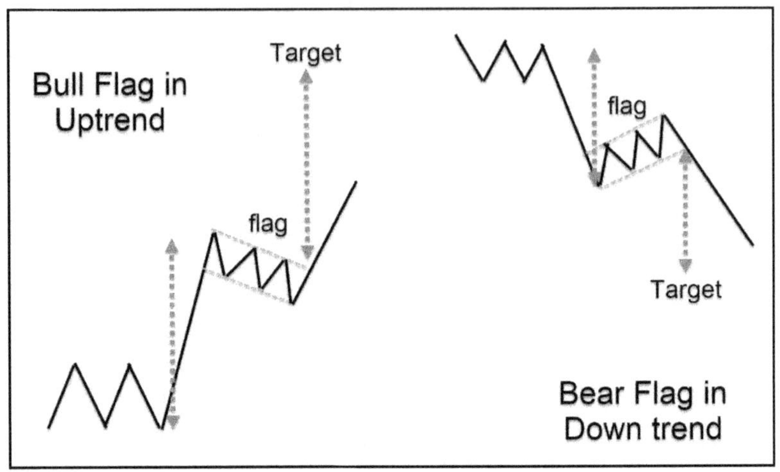

Image 9.12: Flag patterns

Once the flag pattern completes, the price action will typically break out in the direction of the trend that was in place before the pattern formed.

For example, if an uptrend is in place and a bullish flag forms, the price will likely continue increasing after the pattern completes.

Similarly, if a downtrend is in place and a bearish flag forms, the price will likely decrease after the pattern completes.

The breakout from the flag pattern typically occurs on high volume, which confirms that the trend is still in place.

The target for the breakout move can be measured by taking the height of the flagpole (the sharp move higher or lower that occurred before the pattern formed) and adding it to the point at which the breakout occurred.

This gives us a target price we can expect the security to move towards once the flag pattern completes.

Image 9.13 shows an example of a bull flag in Adani Enterprises. This stock was in a strong uptrend and displayed two successive

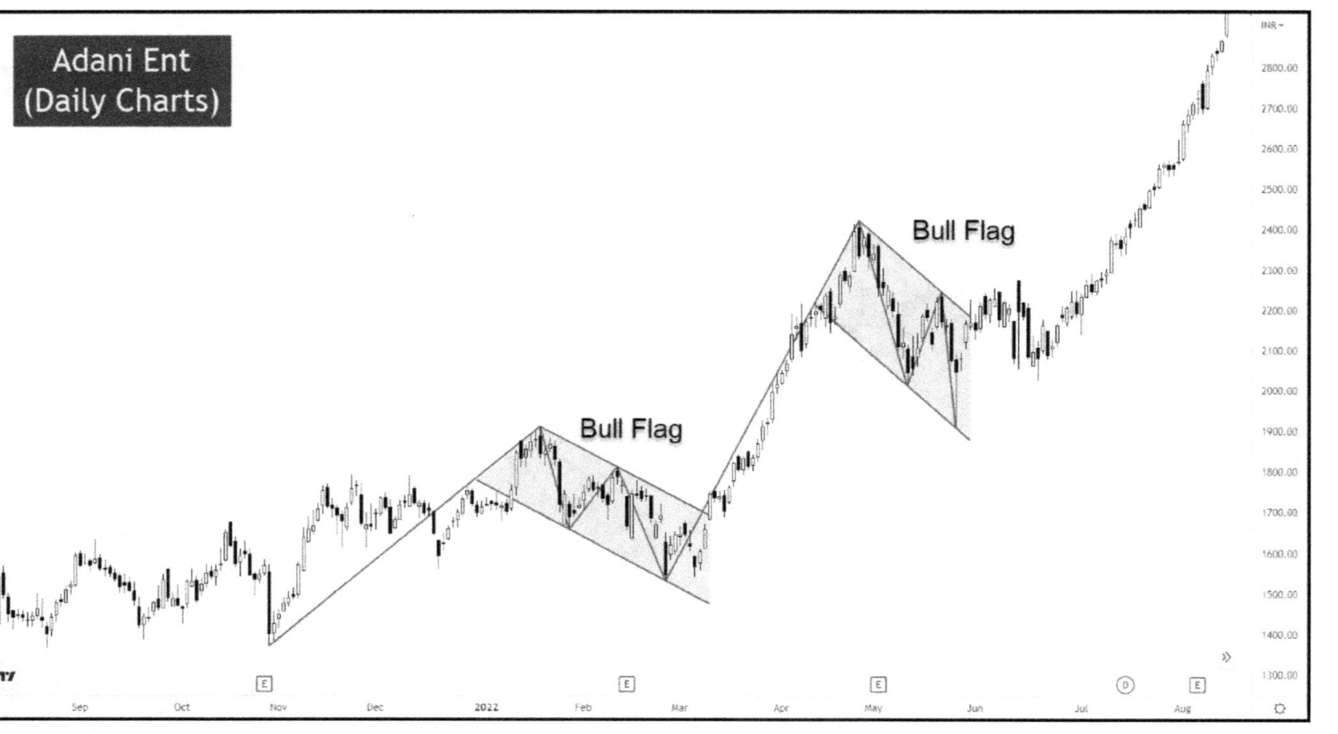

Image 9.13: Bull flag in Adani Enterprises

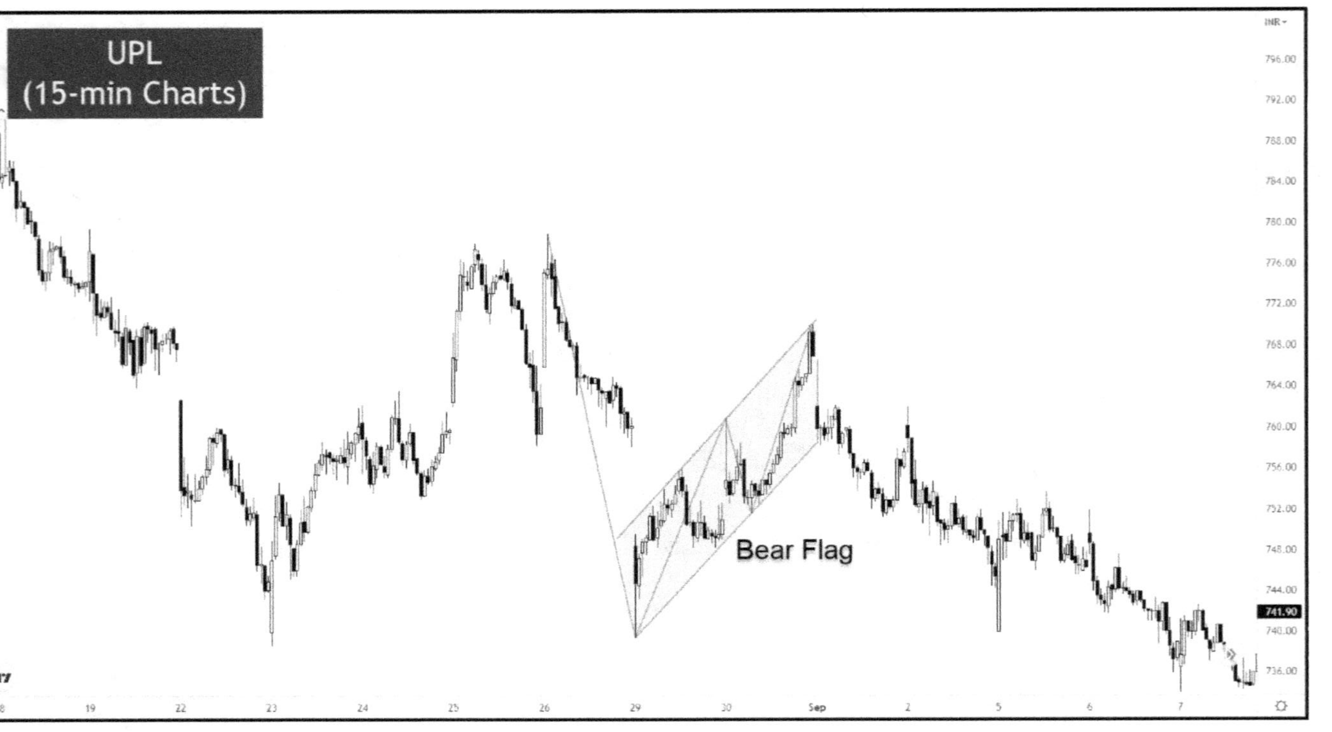

Image 9.14: Bull flag in UPL Ltd.

bull flag patterns and the price rallied further on the upside after the breakout.

Image 9.14 shows an example of a bull flag in UPL Ltd. This stock was in a downtrend and displayed a bear flag pattern, and the price rallied further on the downside after the breakdown.

5. SYMMETRICAL TRIANGLE

Triangles are continuation patterns that show the market is in consolidation before resuming its trend.

This pattern is created when the price forms two converging trend lines, creating a 'triangle' shape.

These trend lines are created by drawing a line from the peak of a recent rally to the trough of a recent pullback and then connecting the previous pullback to the peak of the last rally.

The symmetry in this pattern occurs when the slope of both trend lines is equal. This indicates that bulls and bears are evenly matched and that neither side is able to gain an advantage.

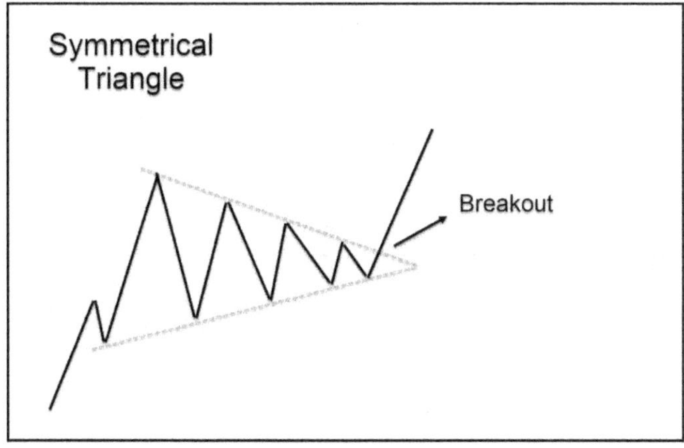

Image 9.15: Symmetrical triangle

As the triangle forms, the trading range narrows, and price volatility decreases. This often leads to a price breakout as the triangle reaches a point.

Traders can use the symmetrical triangle pattern to enter or exit trades.

For example, if the price is trending higher and forms a symmetrical triangle pattern, the traders may look to enter long positions when the price breaks out above the upper trend line.

Likewise, suppose the share price is trending lower and forms a symmetrical triangle pattern, in that case traders may look to enter short positions when the price breaks out below the lower trend line.

Image 9.16 shows an example of a symmetrical triangle pattern in the US Dollar-Japanese Yen chart. The price was in a strong uptrend and displayed a proper symmetrical pattern, and the price rallied further on the upside after the breakout.

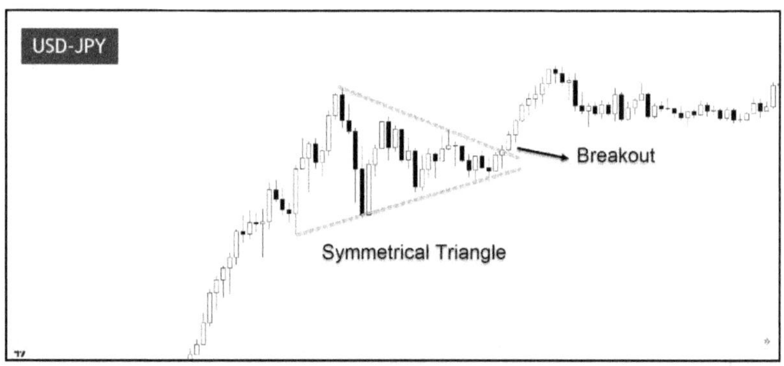

Image 9.16: Symmetrical triangle in US Dollar-Japanese Yen

The key to trading chart patterns successfully is to wait for a breakout from the pattern before entering a trade. For example, if you see a head and shoulders pattern forming after an uptrend, you will wait for the price to break below the neckline (support level) before shorting the stock or currency pair.

Another vital thing to remember when trading chart patterns is that no two patterns are exactly alike. This means that there is no perfect way to trade them. Instead, it is important to use discretion and intuition when making trading decisions.

If you are new to trading, it is always best to practice with a demo account first so that you can get a feel for how to trade chart patterns without risking any real money. Once you have a good understanding of how they work, you can start trading with a live account.

10

THE UNTOLD TRUTH ABOUT CANDLESTICK PATTERNS THAT NOBODY WANTS TO HEAR

Candlestick patterns are one of the most important tools that traders use to predict future price movements. There are a variety of different candlestick patterns that can be used, each with its own interpretation.

Candlestick patterns are a way of representing price data on a chart. They can be used to identify potential reversals in the market. There are many candlestick patterns, but some of the most common ones include engulfing, hammer, shooting star, and doji.

When trying to identify potential reversals using candlestick patterns, it is essential to look at the context of the pattern in relation to the overall trend. For instance, a bullish engulfing pattern at a support trend line is more powerful than the same bullish engulfing pattern in the normal price movement, because a bullish engulfing pattern at a support line implies the participation of big players.

It is also important to remember that no single candlestick pattern is guaranteed to indicate a reversal. Instead, candlestick patterns should be used in conjunction with other technical concepts to give you a complete picture of what is happening in the market.

ENGULFING

The engulfing pattern is a candlestick chart pattern used to predict the reversal of the current trend.

The pattern is composed of two candles, with the first candle being a small candle and the second candle being a large candle.

The key to this pattern is that the second candle completely engulfs the first candle's body. This indicates that there has been a shift in market sentiment.

There are two types of engulfing patterns:

1. Bullish Engulfing
2. Bearish Engulfing

Traders often look for confirmation before entering a trade based on this pattern. The engulfing pattern can be found in any timeframe, but it is most often used on a daily chart.

In **bullish engulfing**, the first candle in the pattern is a small bearish candle, and the second candle is a large bullish candle. The key to this pattern is that the second candle completely engulfs the first candle's body (image 10.1). This indicates that there has been a shift in market sentiment from bearish to bullish.

Image 10.2 shows a bullish engulfing pattern. There was a clear support trend line on the chart, and the bullish engulfing appeared

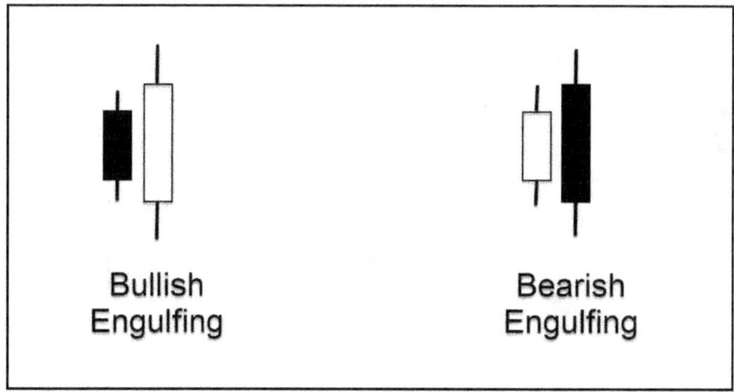

Image 10.1: Engulfing patterns

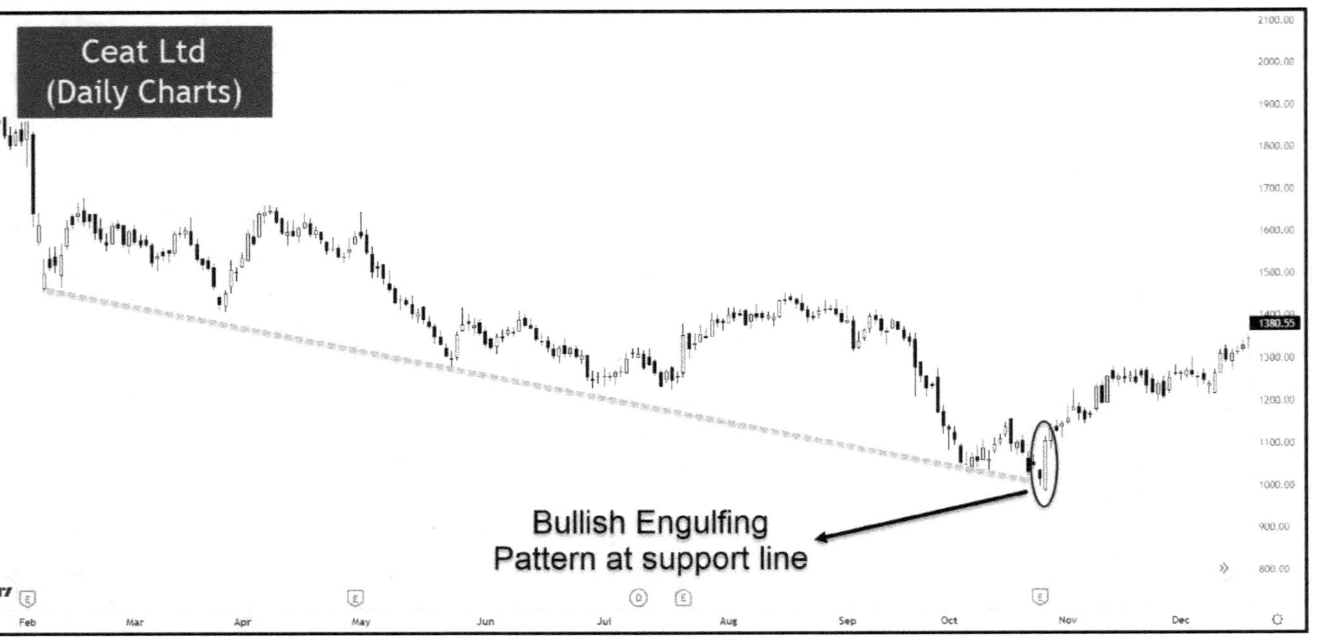

Image 10.2: Bullish engulfing pattern in Ceat Ltd.

exactly at the support line. This indicates the strength of the buyers, and the price rallied on the upside.

Image 10.3 also shows an example of a bullish engulfing pattern. However, it did not appear at the support or resistance trend line, so it doesn't have any impact. Therefore, traders should look at this pattern only at the important price levels or support or resistance trend lines.

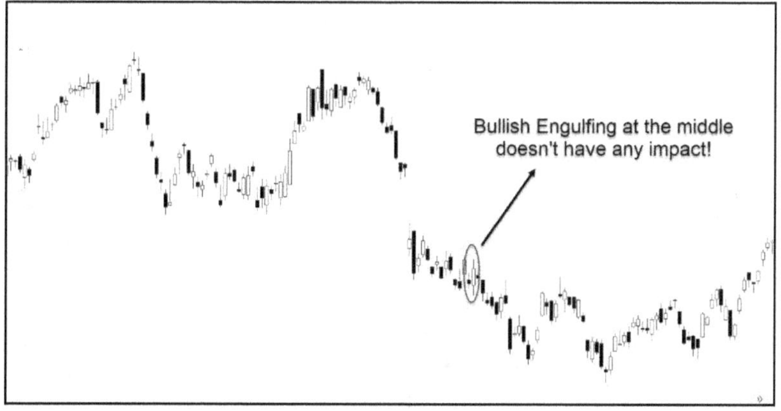

Image 10.3: Bullish engulfing pattern without any impact

Another popular candlestick pattern is the **bearish engulfing pattern**. This pattern occurs when a small white candlestick is followed by a large black candlestick, which completely engulfs the previous day's candlestick.

This pattern indicates that the bulls are losing control and that the bears are taking over. The bearish engulfing pattern is a strong signal that prices will continue moving lower.

Image 10.4 shows an example of a bearish engulfing pattern. There was a clear resistance trend line on the chart, and the bearish

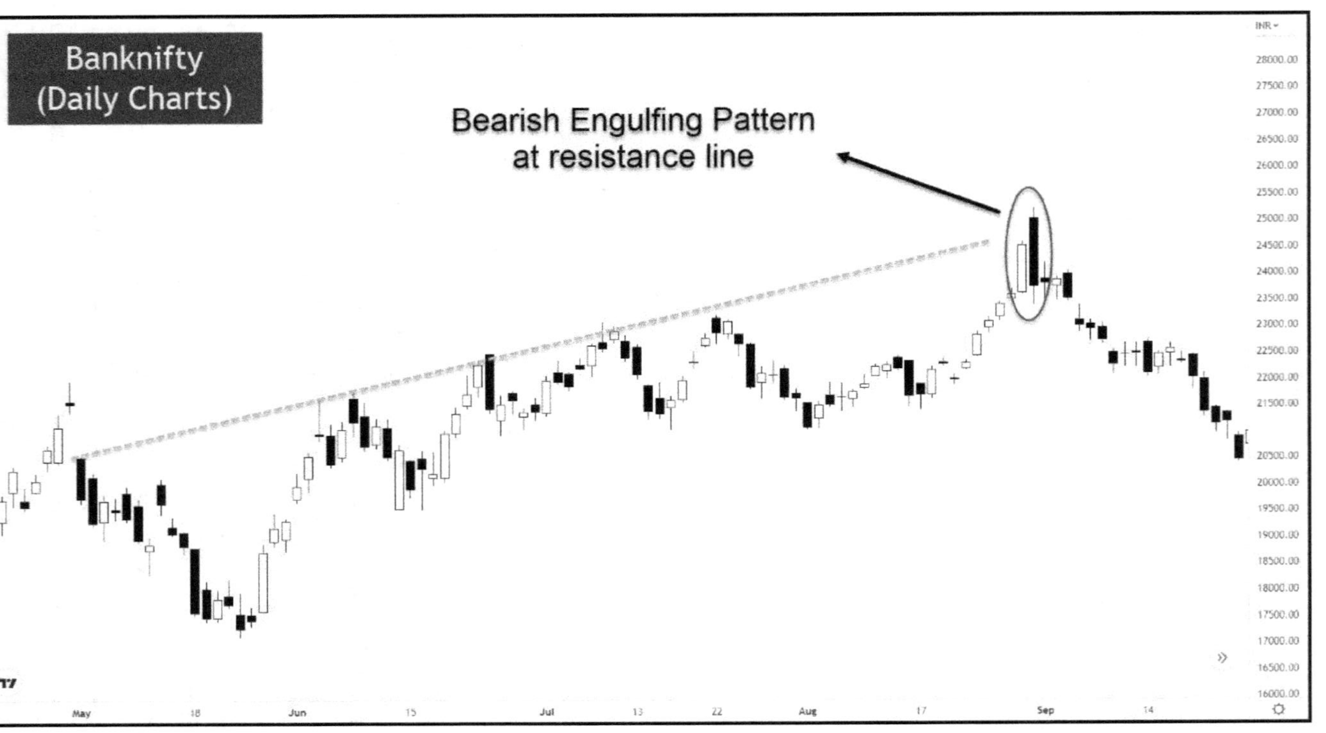

Image 10.4: Bearish engulfing pattern

engulfing appeared exactly at the top of the resistance line. This indicates the strength of the sellers, and the fall of the price later.

Image 10.5 shows an example of a bearish engulfing pattern in Coal India (daily charts). There was a clear resistance trend line on the chart, and the bearish engulfing appeared at the resistance line. This indicates the strength of the sellers. The share price fell later.

Marubozu

The Marubozu candlestick pattern is considered a very reliable signal for forex traders. It is one of the simplest patterns to identify. This pattern consists of a single candle with no wicks, and it is considered to be very bearish or bullish, depending on the context in which it appears (image 10.6).

When the open price is equal to the high price and the close price is equal to the low price, a bearish marubozu forms.

This indicates that selling pressure was intense throughout the entire period and that the prices closed near their lows.

A bullish marubozu forms when the open price is equal to the low price and the close price is equal to the high price. This indicates that buying pressure was intense throughout the entire period, and the prices closed near their highs.

Image 10.7 shows an example of a bullish marubozu pattern in Reliance (daily charts). There was a clear breakout of the resistance trend line on the chart with a bullish marubozu pattern. This indicates the strength of the buyers, and the price rallied upside later.

Image 10.5: Bearish engulfing pattern in Coal India

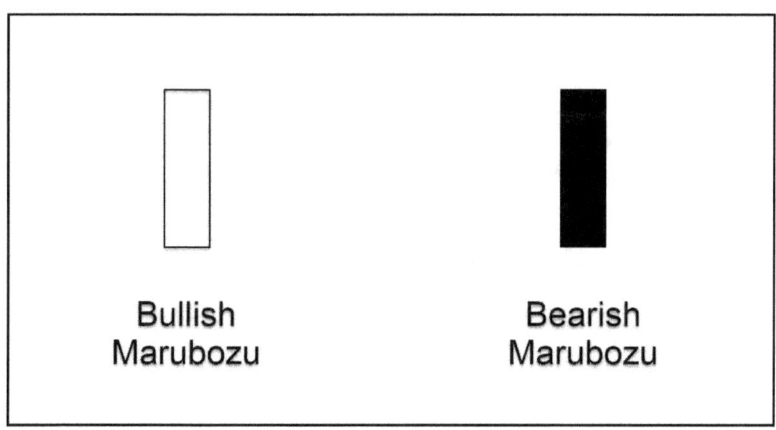

Image 10.6: Marubozu patterns

Image 10.8 shows an example of a bearish marubozu pattern in Tata Power (daily charts). There was an apparent resistance from the price at the resistance trend line with a bearish marubozu pattern. This indicates the strength of the sellers; the price fell later.

The marubozu pattern is considered reliable because it shows a clear and concise picture of market sentiment. This pattern can be found in all timeframes, but it is most commonly used in daily charts. When trading with the marubozu pattern, it is essential to pay attention to the direction of the trend and the context in which the pattern forms. A bearish marubozu in an uptrend may not be as significant as a bearish marubozu in a downtrend.

If you are looking for a simple yet reliable signal, the marubozu candlestick pattern is a good choice. This pattern can help you make well-informed decisions about your trades and can also be used as part of a larger trading strategy.

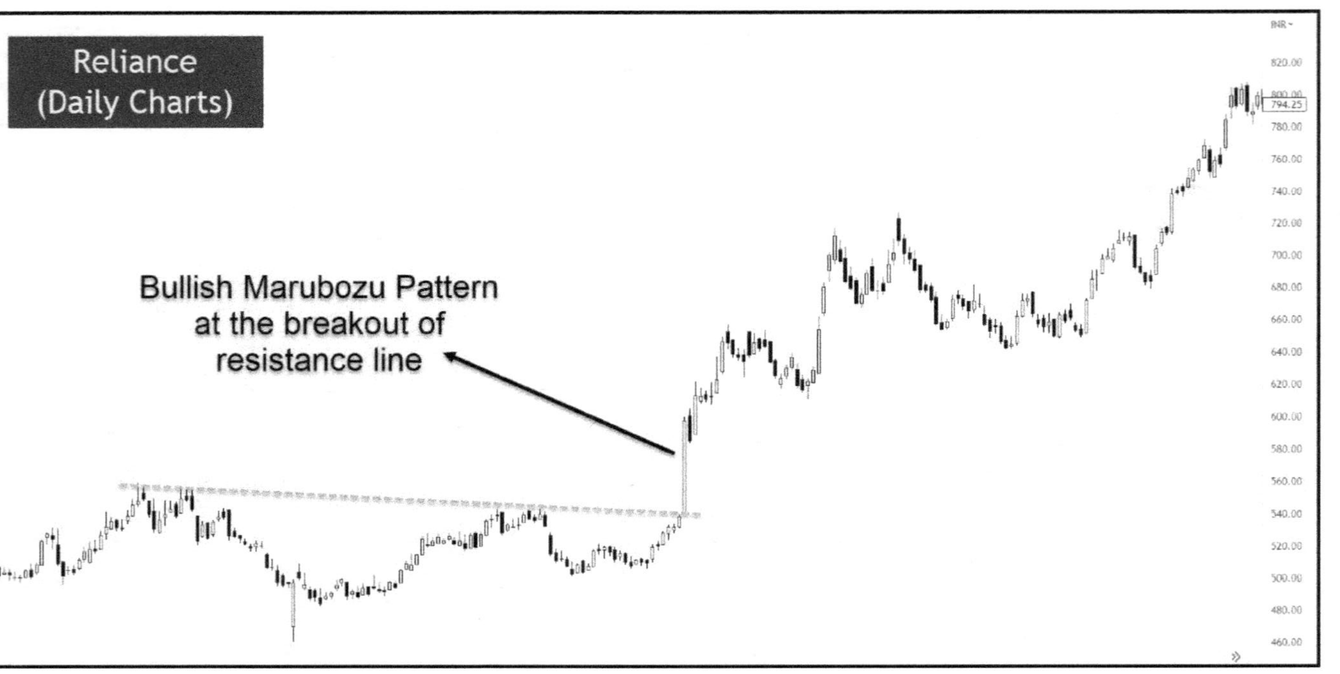

Image 10.7: Bullish marubozu pattern in Reliance

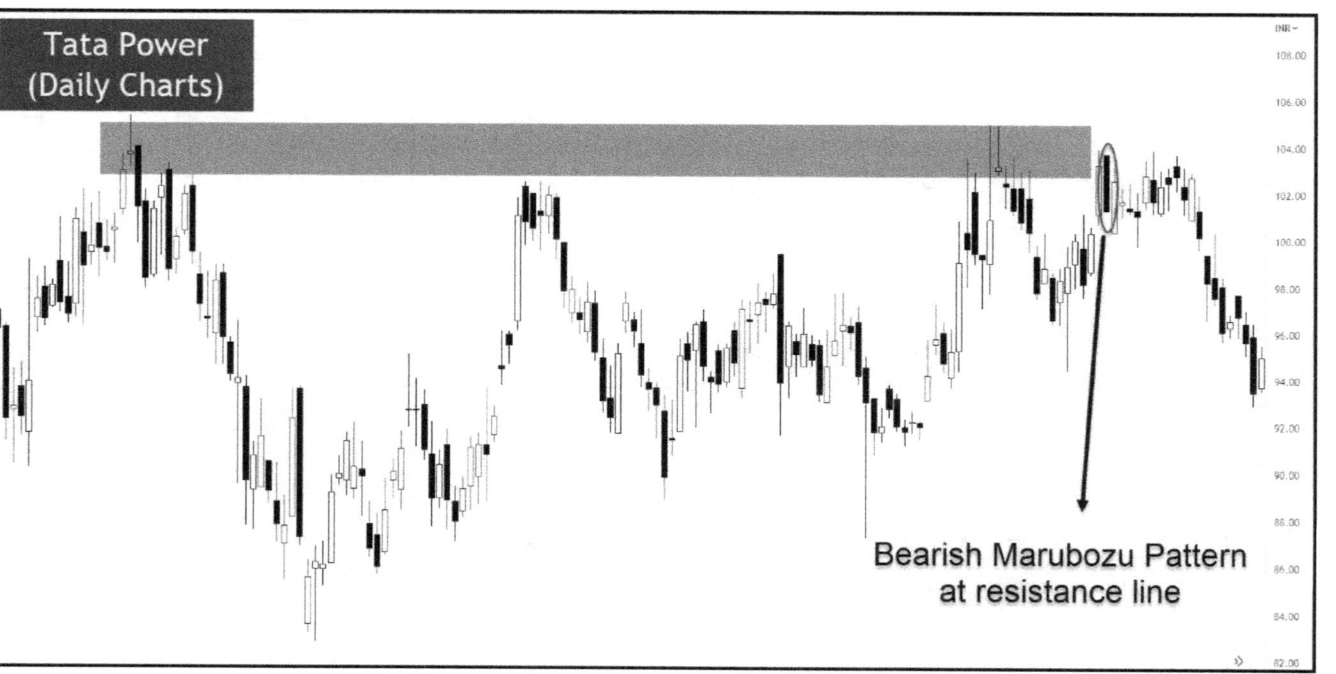

Image 10.8: Bearish marubozu pattern in Tata Power

ABANDONED BABY

This is a candlestick pattern that can be used to predict reversals in the market. The name 'abandoned baby' comes from the fact that this pattern looks like a baby who has been abandoned.

There are two variations–bullish abandoned baby and bearish abandoned baby.

The bullish abandoned baby pattern consists of three candlesticks. The first candlestick is a long black candle, followed by a doji (a candle with a small body and long wicks). The third candle is a white candle that closes above the midpoint of the black candle's body.

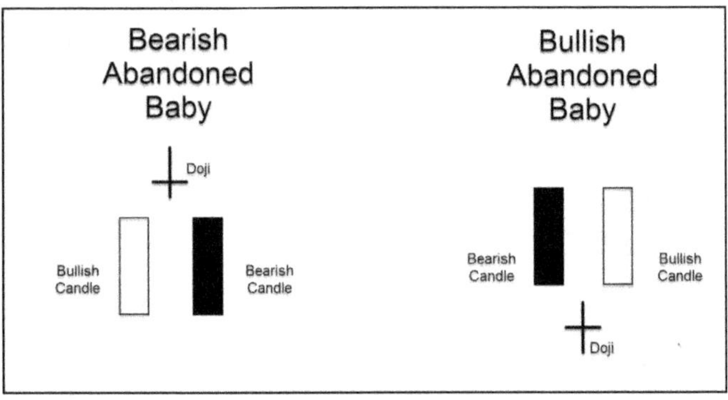

Image 10.9: Abandoned baby patterns

Image 10.10 shows an example of a bearish abandoned baby pattern. The first candle is bullish, followed by a small doji and a bearish candle at the end. Most importantly, it appeared at the resistance line, and the price headed downward later.

Similarly, a bearish abandoned baby pattern consists of three candlesticks. The first candlestick is a long white candle, followed by a doji (a candle with a small body and long wicks). The third

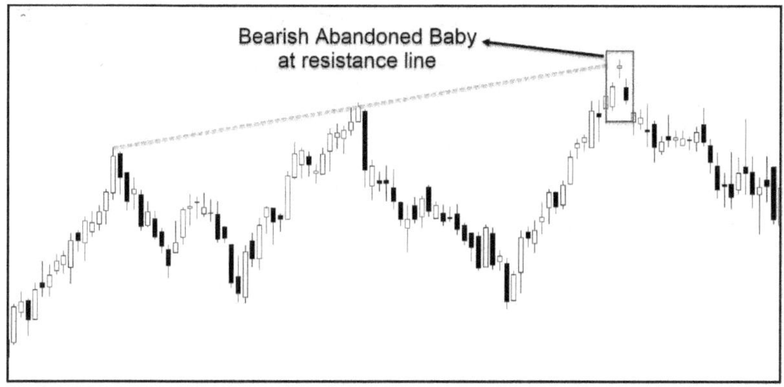

Image 10.10: Bearish abandoned baby pattern

candle is a black candle that closes below the midpoint of the white candle's body.

Image 10.11 shows an example of a bullish abandoned baby pattern. The first candle is a bearish candle, followed by a small doji and a bullish candle at the end. Most importantly, it appeared at the support line, and the price headed upside later.

This pattern is considered a reliable reversal indicator and can be used at any timeframe. However, it is most effective on longer timeframes, such as daily or weekly charts.

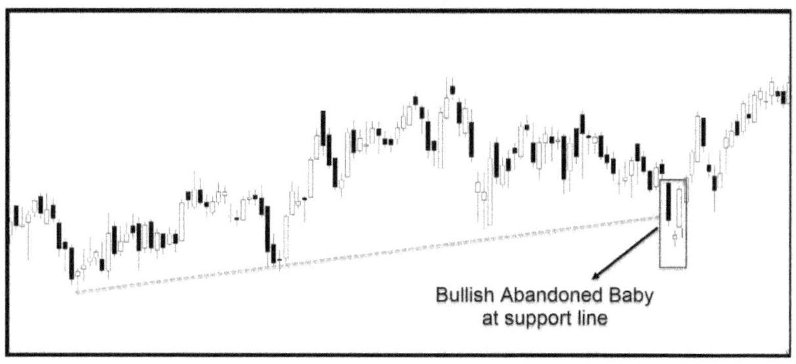

Image 10.11: Bullish abandoned baby pattern

If you see a bullish abandoned baby pattern on a chart, entering a long position (buy) order is a good idea. Your stop-loss should be placed just below the low of the black candle. Your target can be the previous high, or you can exit when you see the first signs of weakness. Similar logic can be used for short trades in the case of a bearish abandoned baby.

Hammer

The hammer pattern occurs when the price moves down significantly during the day but then rallies back to close near the opening price.

Hammer candlestick patterns are reversal patterns that can occur at the bottom of a downtrend. They are created when the open, high, and close prices are roughly equal, but the low price is significantly lower than the other three prices.

This indicates that there was significant selling pressure during the day. Still, buyers were able to push prices back up near the opening level by the end of the day.

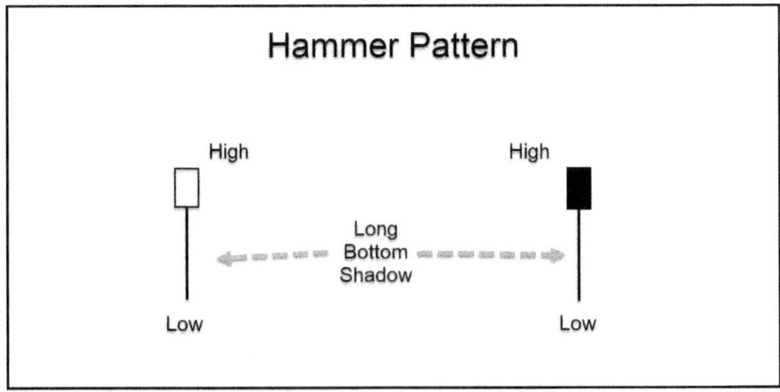

Image 10.12: Hammer pattern

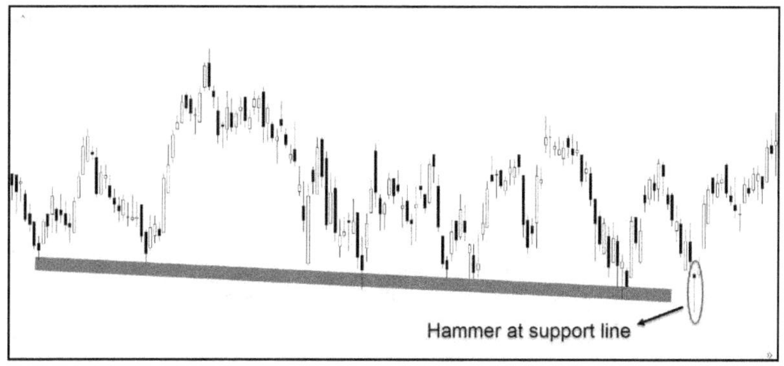

Image 10.13: Hammer pattern at support range

Image 10.13 shows an example of a hammer pattern at the support range. The body is small compared to the long tail. This indicates the presence of strong buyers, and the price rallied upside later.

While hammer candlesticks can occur in any market, they are most common in downtrends. This is because they indicate that sellers are losing control and that buyers may be ready to take over.

If prices continue to move higher after a hammer candlestick forms, it is said to be 'confirmed'. There are many ways to trade hammer candlesticks. However, some of the most common include waiting for confirmation before entering a trade, buying on the open of the next candlestick, and placing stop-loss orders below the low of the hammer candlestick.

SPINNING TOP

The spinning top candlestick pattern is a small candle with a long wick on both sides (image 10.14).

This indicates that there is a lot of indecision in the market and that the bulls and bears are evenly matched. The color of the candle doesn't matter; what matters is the long wicks.

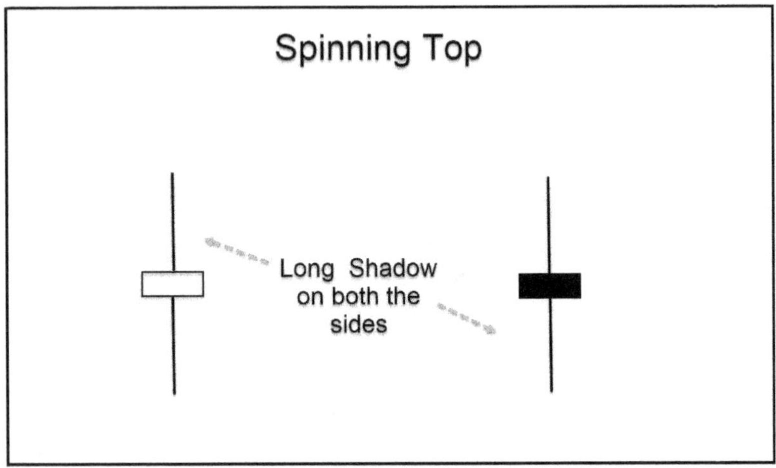

Image 10.14: Spinning top

This pattern can occur at the top or bottom of a trend and signals a potential reversal. When you see this pattern, pay attention to the price action around it and look for confirmation before taking any trades.

Image 10.15 shows an example of a spinning top pattern that occurred at the resistance range. The body is small compared to

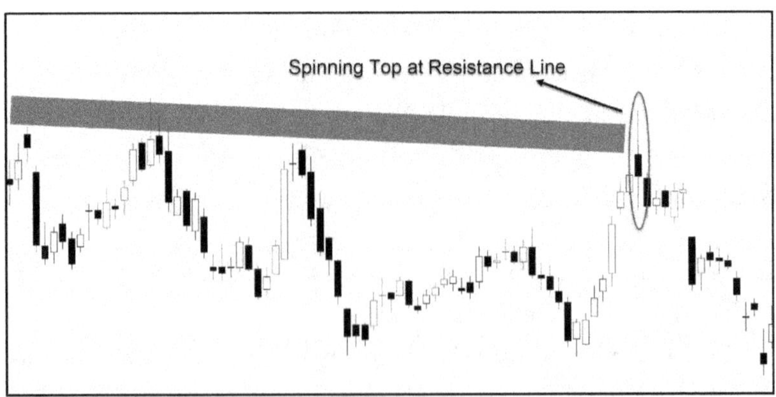

Image 10.15: Spinning top at resistance range

the long tail on both sides. This indicates that indecision at that moment means a fierce fight between buyers and sellers. So, if we have a long position, it is better to exit or trail the stop-loss below the low of the spinning top.

When trading with the help of candlestick patterns, there are a few things to keep in mind to be successful:

1. It is important to identify the key characteristics of each pattern.
2. It is necessary to understand the potential market implications of each formation.
3. It is also crucial to have a sound money management strategy in place before entering any trade.

One of the most important things to remember when trading with candlestick patterns is that they are only one tool in the trader's arsenal. It is essential to use them in conjunction with other technical indicators, such as support and resistance levels, in order to make more informed trading decisions. Additionally, it is also essential to pay attention to the overall market context before making any moves.

11

Here's What No One Tells You About Trading Instruments

In trading, there are three primary instruments used to make trades:

1. Equity,
2. Futures, and
3. Options.

Each trading instrument has its own unique characteristics and risks that must be considered before making any trades.

Equity is the most basic form of trading instrument. It refers to the ownership stake that an investor has in a company.

Equity trading is often considered less risky than other forms of trading, such as futures or options because it represents a direct ownership stake in a company.

When you purchase shares of a company, you become a shareholder and have a claim on that company's assets and profits. However, equity prices can fluctuate slightly and be subject to market volatility.

Future contracts are simple agreements to buy or sell an asset at a future date and price. Futures contracts are used by big investors to hedge against price changes in the underlying asset, or to speculate by the majority of the traders.

For example, if you expect the price of gold to increase, you could purchase a gold futures contract. If the price of gold does indeed rise, you will make a profit on your contract. However, if the price of gold decreases, you will incur a loss.

Future contracts are considered riskier than equity because one lot of futures contracts can get you more shares.

Options are similar to futures as they are agreements to buy or sell an asset at a future date and price. However, options give the buyer the right but not the obligation to make the trade. This means that if the price of the underlying asset moves in the desired direction, the option holder can make a profit. However, if the price moves in the opposite direction, the option holder will lose the initial investment.

Options selling can increase the accuracy, but less reward per trade decreases drastically. Besides, it also brings the unlimited loss scenario (in case of no hedging or stop-loss) to the table.

Also, other factors (greeks, explained later in the chapter in the section 'Factors which affect the option premium') can also affect the option's value. Because of these reasons, options are considered to be even riskier than futures.

Let's consider an example and explore how the risk-reward varies in these instruments.

There are three traders: 'E', 'F,' and 'O'.

All of them have Rs. 1,50,000 as their trading capital. Besides, they all have a bullish view (expect prices to go up) on Tech Mahindra (TECHM) on 9 September 2022 (before the market opens).

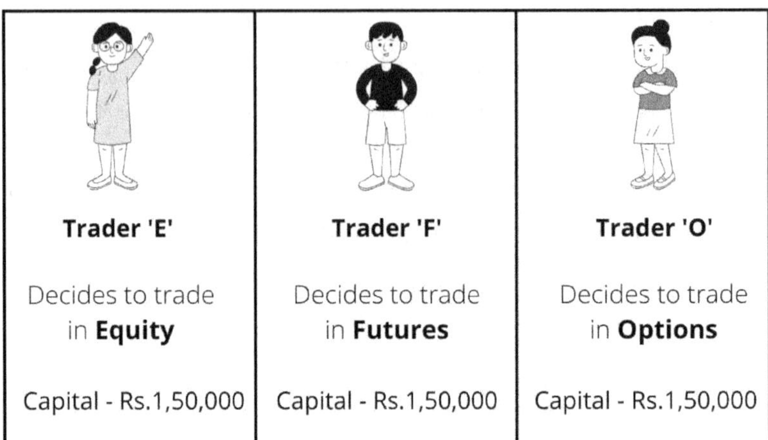

Indian market opens at 9.15 a.m. There is a bullish engulfing pattern at the support line at 10.45 a.m. So, it confirms their view, and therefore, all plan to take a long trade.

Trader **E** decides to take the trade in **equities**.

Trader **F** decides to take the trade in **futures**.

Trader **O** decides to take the trade in **options**.

The closing price of TECHM at 10.45 a.m. is Rs. 1090.

Trader E buys **137 shares** (Rs. 1,50,000 capital/CMP 1090).

Trader F buys **1 future lot of TECHM (1 lot = 600 shares, and Rs.1,50,000 is enough to buy 1 lot at this price).**

Trader O decides to buy 1120 CE (call options). The price of 1120 CE at 10.45 a.m. is 21.80. So, he will get 6,600 quantities (11 lots of 1120 CE).

Let's assume all three traders decide to close the trade at 3.00 p.m.

TECHM price at 3.00 p.m. is Rs. 1128.8.

The calculations for all three traders are as follows:

Trader E

Entry price: 1090
Closing price: 1128.8
Profits made = **Rs. 5,315** (38.8 × 137 shares) that is, 3.5% returns on capital.

Trader F

Entry price: 1090
Closing price: 1128.8
Profits made = **Rs. 23,280** (38.8 × 600 shares) i.e., 15.5% returns on capital.
(*Note:* Values will be slightly different in the TECHM futures chart. But we have used the spot values for easy calculation)

Trader O

Entry price: 1090 (1120 CE entry at 21.8)
Closing price: 1128.8 (1120 CE exit at 43)
Profits made = **Rs.1,39,920** (21.2 × 6600 shares) that is, 93.2% returns on capital.

Please note that this is a simple cherry-picked example to illustrate the different degrees of risk-reward offered by these trading instruments.

Instead of the price moving in our expected direction, if it moves in the opposite direction, Trader E will also lose less money, Trader F will lose some more money, and Trader O will lose more capital.

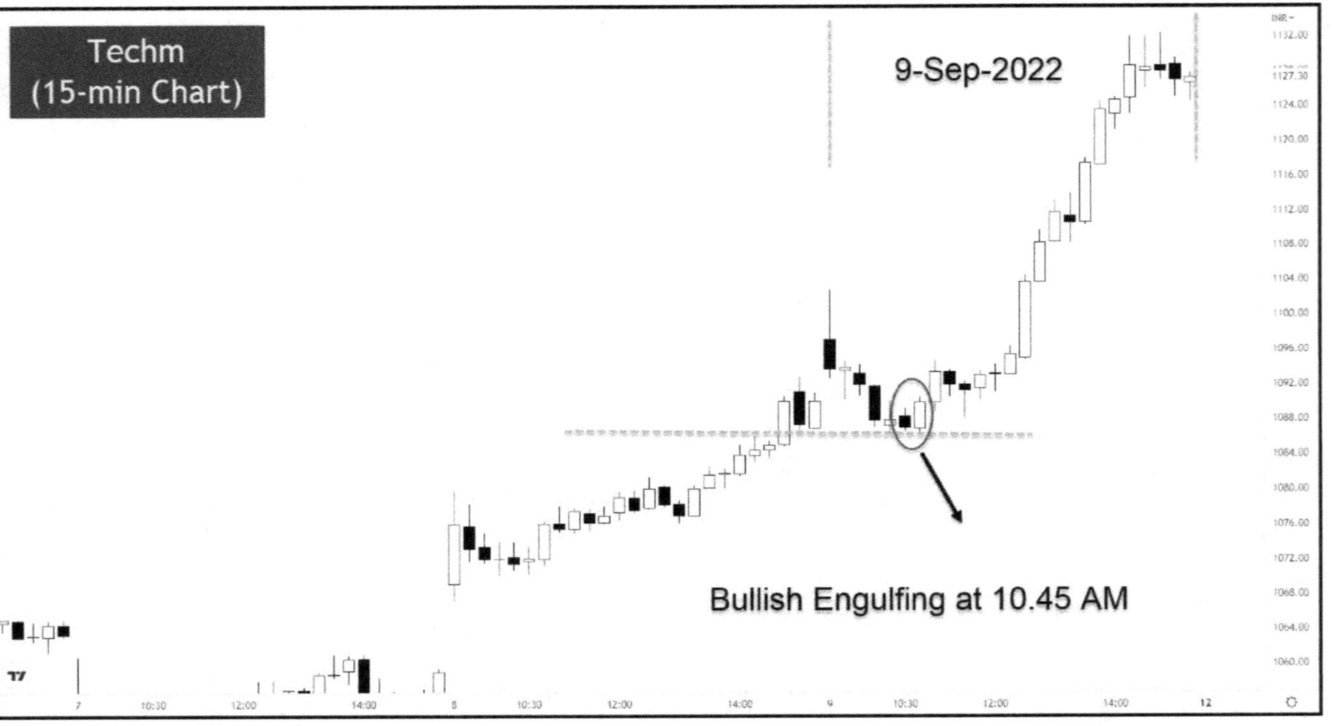

Image 11.1: TECHM chart on 9 September 2022

Image 11.2: TECHM 1120 CE chart

TRADING IN FUTURES

Futures is a double-edged sword that simply amplifies your trading results. In the above case, Trader F was right, and hence made 15.5% returns on his capital in one day.

But what if his view was wrong? What if TECHM displayed the same movement on the downside?

He would have lost 15.5% of his capital in one day!

Traders can take the below precautions before trading in futures:

1. Follow one trading system

By finalizing one trading system and doing rigorous testing of past scenarios, traders can develop high conviction in their chosen system and profit from trading futures.

Rigorous testing of past scenarios allows traders to understand how their system would have performed in the past across different market conditions and thereby helps them ascertain whether the system is robust enough to generate profits in the future.

Such results can also help traders gauge their risk and reward profile and make necessary adjustments to improve their chances of success.

2. Stop-loss is a must

When trading futures, it is important to always use a technical stop-loss to protect your capital.

A technical stop-loss is a predetermined point at which you will sell a security if it begins to move in the wrong direction to prevent further losses.

For instance, in the above example (image 11.1), let us assume the price fell instead of going upside. If Trader F had the stop-loss below the support trend line (that is, 1085), then he would lose only Rs. 3,000 instead of Rs. 23,280.

By using a stop-loss, you can ensure that you never lose more money than you are comfortable with losing.

3. Risk only 2% of capital on each trade

When making profits in futures trading, the most important thing you can do is make sure that you're only risking 2% of your capital on each trade.

By doing this, you'll ensure that even if you have a losing streak, you'll still have enough money left to keep trading and eventually recover your losses.

4. Don't ignore gap opening

There are a few things to consider when trading futures to make profits. One is the gap open, which can work against you if you are carrying positions overnight.

What if you carry some positions in futures overnight, and there is a massive gap against your trade the next day? It is vital to be aware of this and factor it into your trading plan.

5. Trading psychology

Maintaining good trading psychology during the trading window is crucial to profit in futures trading. This means avoiding greed and panic, focusing on the plan instead of the profits or losses, and keeping your composure even in difficult situations.

Remember that successful futures traders are not always right, but they always manage their losses well. So be disciplined in your approach, focus on risk management, and stay rational during all market conditions. Doing so will put you in a better position to achieve profitability in futures trading.

Trading in Options

In options trading, there are two key concepts that traders need to be aware of—puts (PE) and calls (CE).

Both put and call options are contracts that give the buyer the right, but not the obligation, to buy or sell an underlying asset at a specified price within a specific timeframe. Put options give the holder the right to sell the asset, while call options give the holder the right to buy the asset.

When it comes to options, there are two key players: the buyer and the seller.

The person who buys an option is said to be the 'long' option (or option buyer), while the person who sells (or 'writes') the option is said to be 'short' (option seller).

Here's a quick rundown of what each player does:

The buyer pays a premium to the seller for the right, but not the obligation, to buy (or sell) a security at a predetermined price within a specified time period.

The seller collects a premium from the buyer upfront in exchange for agreeing to buy or sell a security at a predetermined price within a specified time period.

If the buyer exercises their option, the seller must then fulfill their end of the deal by buying or selling the security at the agreed-upon price.

If the buyer does not exercise their option, the seller gets to keep the premium as profit.

The trade in image 11.2 was an option buying trade. If there was a person who sold 1120 CE to Trader O (assuming he had the short view), and he closed only at the end, then he would lose the same amount! (that is, Rs.1,39,920).

That's why I always insist on understanding options before trading with them.

Buying Options vs. Selling Options

An options buyer pays a premium in advance to have the right to buy or sell an underlying asset, depending on whether they bought a call or put option.

An option seller is someone who receives a premium as payment for giving up their right to the underlying asset until the expiration date.

There are some benefits of options buying.

1. It can be done with small capital.
2. It has the potential to make quick returns.
3. The risk involved is only the premium paid while taking the trade.

But there are some disadvantages of options buying.

1. Accuracy is less as options buyers make money only when the market trends.
2. Time decay decreases the premium.

Now let's see how options selling works.

Benefits of options selling

1. High accuracy as time decay works in favor of sellers.
2. Sellers make a profit even when the price moves sideways.

There are some disadvantages with options selling as well.

1. Sellers can lose big money quickly if the price moves in the opposite direction.

2. Risk-reward is limited in most cases.
3. It demands significant capital.

When it comes to options buying versus options selling, there is no easy answer as to which one is better. It depends on various factors, including your investment goals and objectives, risk tolerance, and overall financial situation.

If you are a person who feels comfortable with high accuracy and small profits, then options selling is good for you.

But if you are okay with taking more risks, don't lose your emotional balance even after facing failures. If you aim to make quick money, then options buying is the right choice for you.

If you are still unsure, spend some time studying options in depth, take some paper trades with options, and then you will get the clarity.

Factors Which Affect Options Premium

The options greeks are the factors that affect the price of an option. The most crucial factor is the underlying asset's price, which is denoted by the letter S. Other important factors include:

- The strike price (K).
- The time to expiration (T).
- The volatility of the underlying asset (σ).
- The interest rate (r).

The Greek letter **delta** measures the change in an option's price with respect to a change in the underlying asset's price. Delta can be either positive or negative, ranging from 0 to 1 for call options and from -1 to 0 for put options.

For example, consider a call option with a delta of 0.50 and an underlying asset with a current price of $50. If the underlying asset's price increases by $1, then the option's price will increase by $0.50 (0.50 × $1).

The Greek letter **gamma** measures the change in delta with respect to a change in the underlying asset's price.

Gamma is always positive for both call and put options, ranging from 0 to infinity.

For example, consider a call option with a delta of 0.50 and a gamma of 0.20. If the underlying asset's price increases by $1, then the option's delta will increase by 0.20 (0.20 × $1), and the new delta will be 0.70.

The Greek letter **vega** measures the change in an option's price with respect to a change in the underlying asset's volatility.

Vega is always positive for both call and put options, ranging from 0 to infinity.

For example, consider a call option with a vega of 0.20 and an underlying asset with current volatility of 20%. If the underlying asset's volatility increases by 1%, then the option's price will increase by $0.20 (0.20 × 1%).

The Greek letter **theta** measures the change in an option's price with respect to a change in the time to expiration. Theta is negative for both call and put options, ranging from -infinity to 0.

For example, consider a call option with a theta of -0.50 and an expiration date that is one month away. If the expiration date is moved down by one day, then the option's price will decrease by $0.50 (-0.50 × 1).

The Greek letter **rho** measures the change in an option's price with respect to a change in the interest rate. Rho is positive for call options and negative for put options, ranging from -infinity to infinity.

For example, consider a call option with a rho of 0.50 and an underlying asset with a current interest rate of 5%. If the interest rate increases by 1%, then the option's price will increase by $0.50 (0.50 × 1%).

In summary, the options greeks are the factors that affect the price of an option. The most important factor is the underlying asset's price, which is denoted by the letter S. Other important factors include the strike price (K), the time to expiration (T), the volatility of the underlying asset (σ), and the interest rate (r).

Covered Call Options Strategy

The covered call options strategy is a popular options trading strategy that involves buying underlying security and selling a call option on the same security. The trade is considered 'covered' because the trader owns the underlying security, which in theory, should cover any losses incurred if the stock price declines.

There are many benefits to using this strategy. One of the main advantages is that it can help to generate income on a stock that might otherwise be stagnant. Covered calls are also relatively low risk compared to other options strategies, which makes them ideal for new or inexperienced options traders.

Let's take an example to understand it better.

Assume an investor holds 250 shares of Reliance in his portfolio. He thinks this stock has a bright future in the long run and plans to keep it for 5 to 10 years.

Instead of simply holding these shares, he can generate monthly returns from his investment.

Let's have a look at the Reliance chart.

If you observe image 11.3, Reliance stock is in a decent uptrend but faces a strong resistance between 2755-2855 levels.

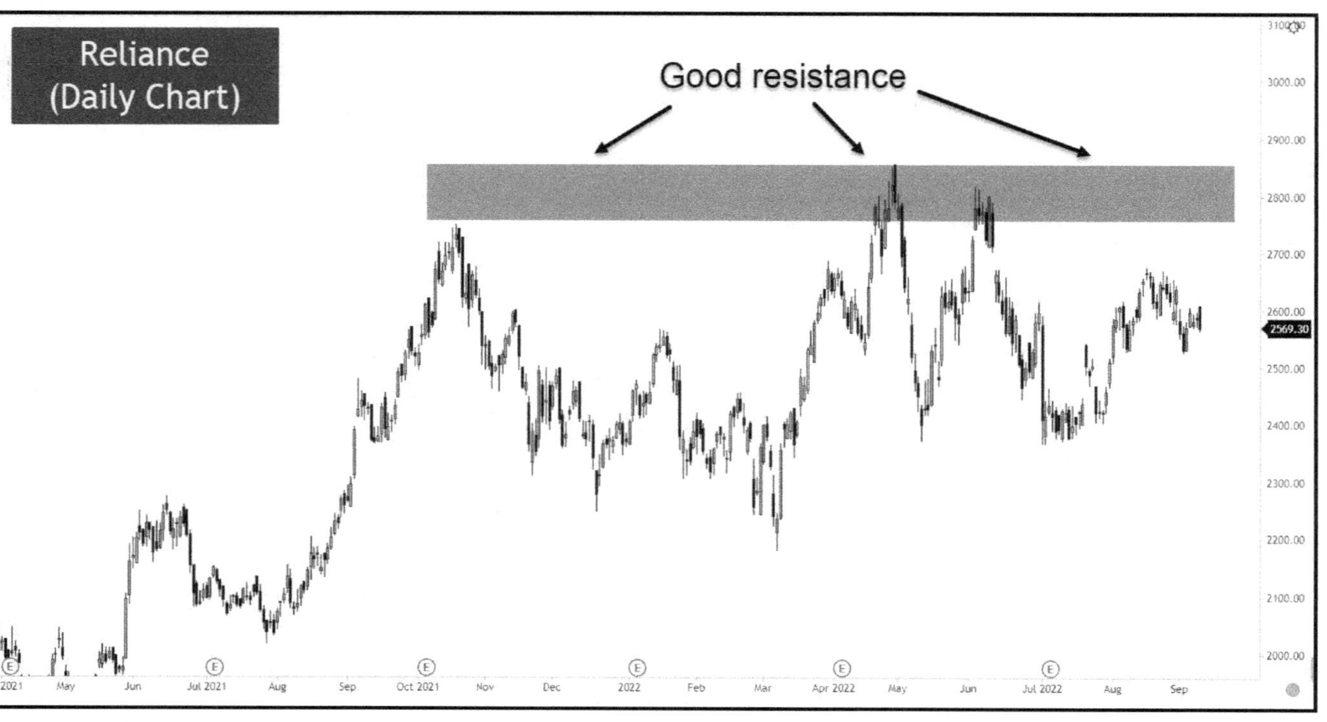

Image 11.3: Reliance daily chart

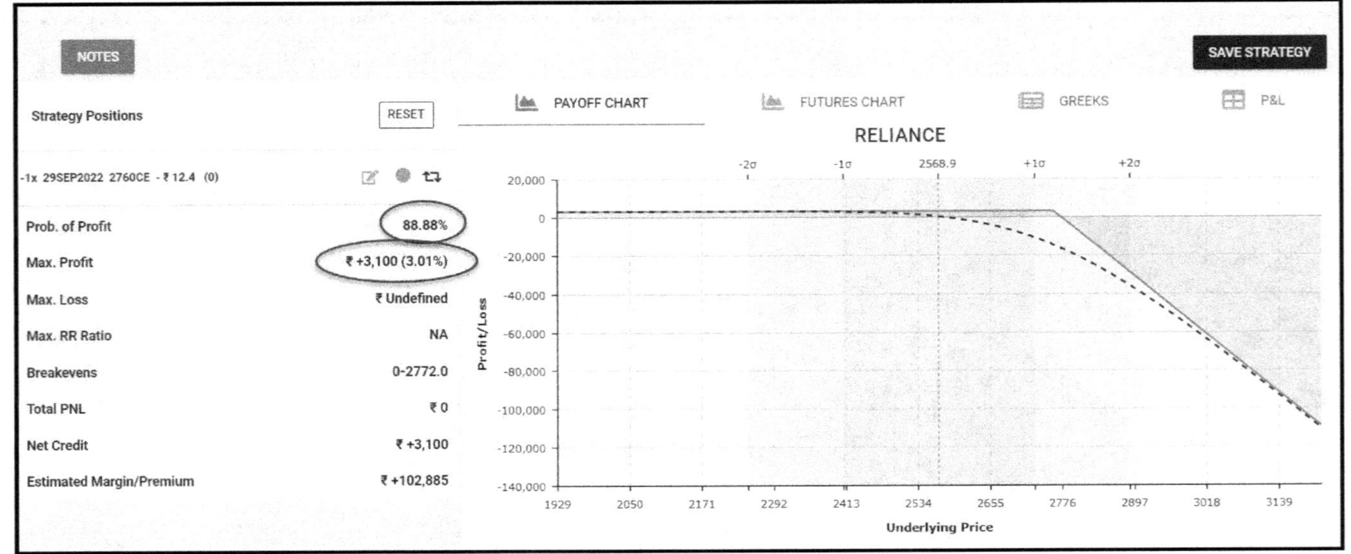

Image 11.4: Payoff chart for Reliance covered call strategy

At the time of writing this piece, only 14 days remain for this monthly expiry.

What is the probability of the price breaking above this resistance zone in the next 14 trading days? It is a rare probability.

So, this investor can sell any call option (CE) at or above this resistance zone and pocket the premium.

Image 11.4 shows a payoff chart for Reliance covered call when the investor sells CE of 2760.

The probability of profit is 89%. It means there is a high probability of making profits, and the maximum profit is Rs. 3,100 for this month.

In this way, this investor can sell the CE every month to generate some monthly income.

He will lose money only if the price closes above 2760 (which is rare). A safe investor can sell further away call options (like 2780 CE or 2300 CE).

This investor will face the loss only when the price closes above his sold strike price. Even in that case, his profits from 250 Reliance shares will compensate for the losses.

The covered call strategy is most effective when used on stocks that are not expected to make big moves in the foreseeable future. This is because the trade aims to generate income from the premium of the call option rather than from the price appreciation of the underlying stock. For this reason, many traders use technical analysis to help them find stocks that are trading in a range or that have recently pulled back from an uptrend.

Once you have placed your orders, you will need to wait until expiration to see if your trade is profitable. Suppose the stock price is below the call option's strike price at expiration. In that case, the option will expire worthlessly, and you will keep the entire premium as profit. If the stock price is above the call option's strike price at expiration, then the option will be exercised, and you will be required to sell your shares at the strike price.

The covered call strategy can be a profitable way to trade options, but it is important to understand the risks involved before implementing this strategy. One of the most significant risks is that you could miss out on potential profits if the underlying security experiences a sudden surge in price. For this reason, it is important to have a well-defined exit strategy before entering any covered call trade.

Vertical Spread

Assume you are planning to take a long trade in an index using options. You have two simple options:

1. Call buy means you buy CE, or
2. Put sell means you sell PE

However, these two have their own disadvantages.

Call buy is profitable only if the price shows a quick move on the upside. Otherwise, the CE premium will come down due to the time decay impact, and you will not be able to hold this trade if the price displays a sideways move.

Put sell looks like a good option as time decay works in its favor. But it brings some risk to the table. For example, what if the price starts going down, and you cannot place the stop-loss order? It can create a big dent in your capital. Because of this risk, margin requirements are also high for options selling.

Is there any way to negate these disadvantages and still take trades with options?

Image 11.5: Nifty 5-minute chart on 4 October 2022

Yes! And credit spread is the answer to this question.

Let us take an example to understand this.

In image 11.5, on 4 October 2022, Nifty displayed a gap up open, and buyers are strong in the first two candles.

At 11.00 a.m., the price gives a small pullback, and now you are interested in taking a trade through options.

Case 1: CE buying

The nearest at-the-money (ATM) strike price is 17200.
Nifty 17200 CE was trading at 100.

If you look at image 11.6, it is evident that Nifty 17200 CE was trading at 100.

At 3.15 p.m., it was trading around 130 (assuming we close 15 minutes before the market closes to avoid last minute volatile moves).

The profit made is around 30 points.

Capital required for 1 lot: Rs. 5,000 (50 Qty/Lot X Rs.100 premium)

Profit per lot: Rs. 1,500

Please note, Nifty displayed a strong upward movement on this day, so the premium of Nifty 17200 CE didn't erode much.

Case 2: PE Selling

The nearest ATM strike price is 17200.
Nifty 17200 PE was trading at 88.

If you look at image 11.7, it is evident that Nifty 17200 PE was trading at 88.

At 3.15 p.m., it was trading around the 57.8 level.

The profit made is around 30.2 points.

Capital required for 1 lot: Rs. 1,00,000 (approximate)

Profit per lot: Rs. 1,510

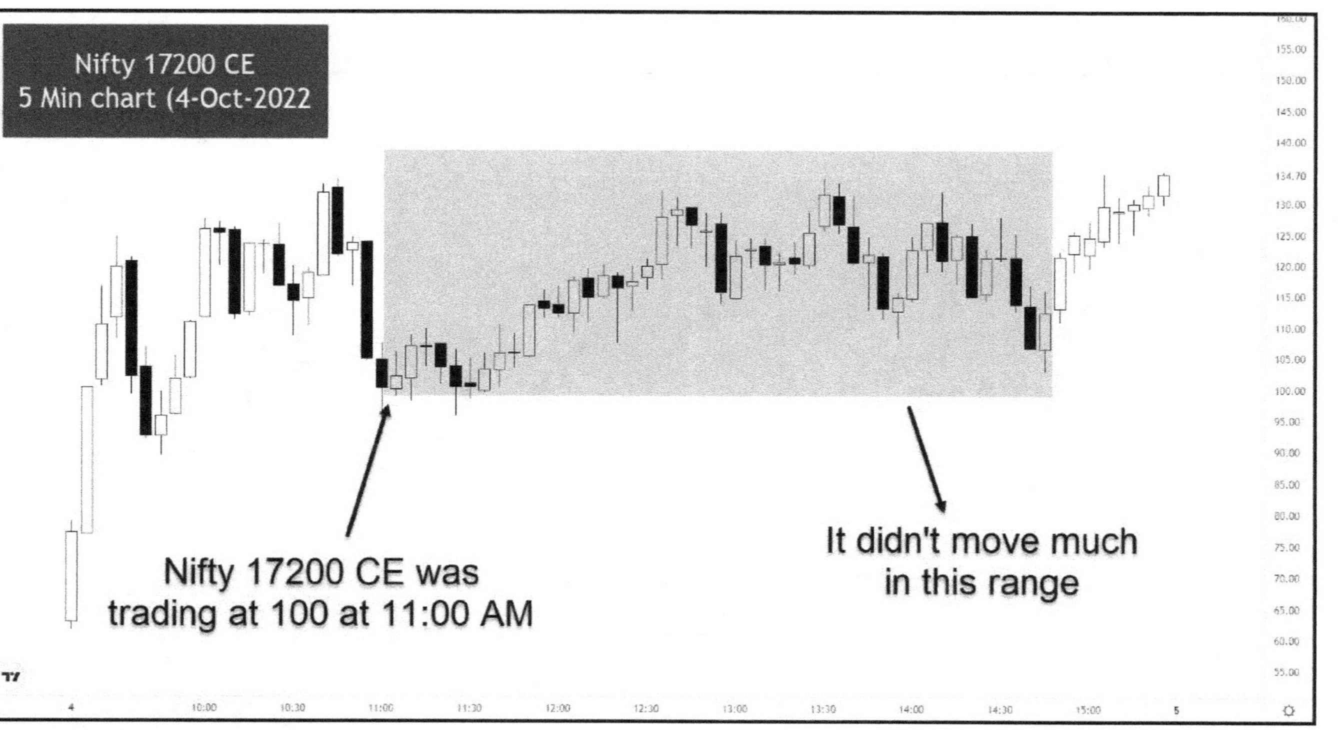

Image 11.6: Nifty 17200 CE 5-minute chart on 4 October 2022

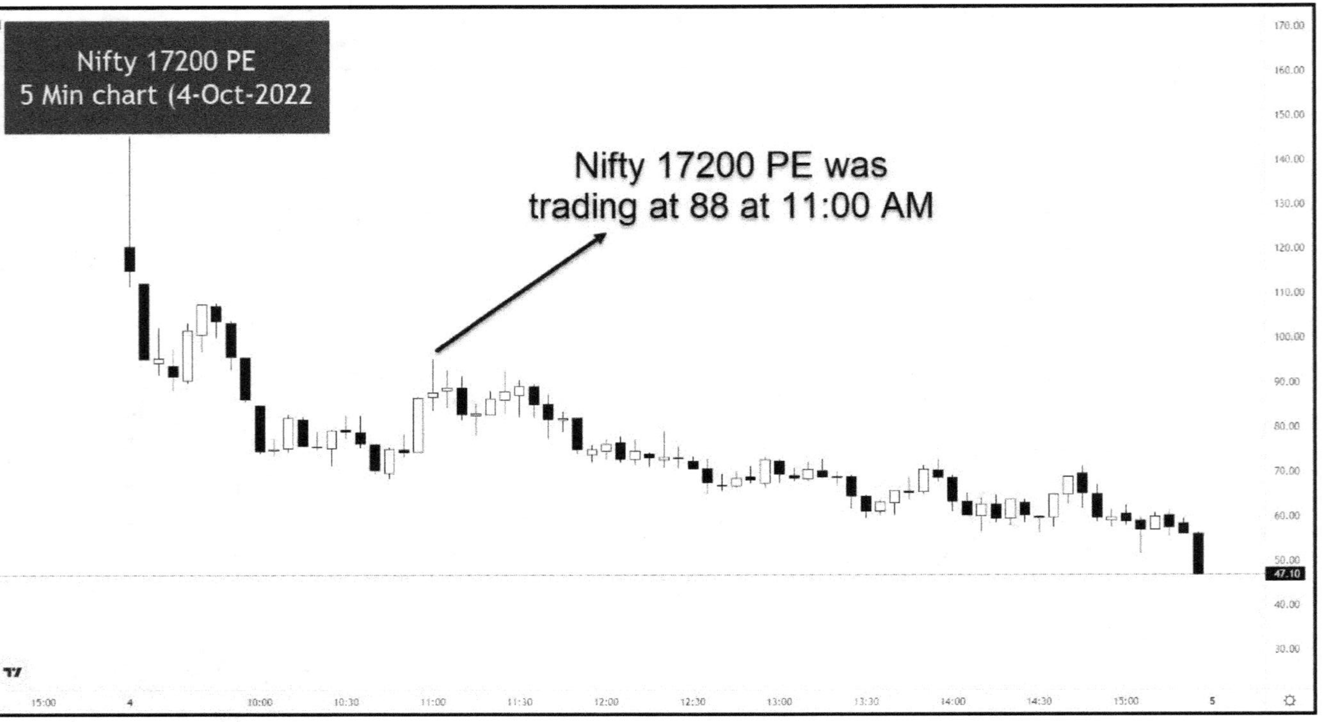

Image 11.7: Nifty 17200 PE 5-minute chart on 4 October 2022

Case 1 is prone to time decay, and case 2 demands more capital. Looking for a spread that protects from time decay and requires less capital is always better.

Case 3: Credit Spread

The nearest ATM strike price is 17200.

As per this strategy, we buy 17200 PE and sell 16900 PE.

At 11:00 a.m.

17200 PE was trading at 85.7

16900 PE was trading at 15.7

At 3.15 p.m.

17200 PE was trading at 57.4

16900 PE was trading at 10.3

It means 17200 PE made a profit of 28.3 (85.7–57.4) and 16900 PE made a loss of 5.4 (15.7–10.3).

So the total profit is 22.9 points.

Capital required for 1 lot: Rs. 32,000 (approximate)

Profit per lot: Rs. 1,145

If you check carefully, credit spread takes less capital to execute the same trade. Besides, it also provides protection against time decay.

12

HOW OPEN INTEREST HELPS YOU IMPROVE TRADING

Open interest (OI) is the number of outstanding (pending) contracts, including short and long positions, held by market participants at the end of the day. It is a good indicator of market activity, liquidity, and the level of participation in a particular market. We can use OI to identify market trends and confirm or deny the signals with other technical indicators. In general, high levels of OI indicate a large number of market participants and strong demand or supply for the underlying asset.

When trading, it is always important to keep an eye on OI levels so that you can make informed decisions about your trades. If you see high levels of OI, it indicates that the market is ripe with opportunity. Suppose you see low levels of OI, it may indicate that the market is not currently offering much in the way of opportunity. Either way, tracking OI can give you valuable insights into the current state of the market.

OI vs. Volume

OI is the total number of contracts outstanding in a futures market. It is a measure of market activity and liquidity.

Volume is the total number of contracts traded during a given period. It is a measure of market activity but not necessarily liquidity.

The difference between OI and volume is simple. OI represents the number of contracts that are currently open. In contrast, the volume represents the total number of contracts traded during a given period.

OI can give you an idea of how liquid a market is, while volume can give you an idea of how active it is.

Let's take an example to understand the difference between OI and volume in a better manner.

Assume XYZ stock is listed in the futures and options space, and hence market participants can take the trade in the futures and options category.

On the first day, the OI of XYZ futures was zero.

Ram buys 1 lot of futures, thinking XYZ price will go up. At the same time, Sham sells 1 lot of futures, hoping the XYZ price will fall.

After the first day:

Day	Activity	OI Change	Total OI
	Ram Buys 1 lot		
1	Sham Sells 1 lot	1	1

On the second day, John buys 3 lots, and Tom sells 3 lots of XYZ futures.

After the second day:

Day	Activity	OI Change	Total OI
1	Ram Buys 1 lot Sham Sells 1 lot	1	1
2	John Buys 3 lots Tom Sells 3 lots	3	4

On the third day, Ram sells his 1 lot (which he bought on the first day), and Tom buys 1 lot (reduces his short position, which he opted on the second day).

After the third day:

Day	Activity	OI Change	Total OI
1	Ram Buys 1 lot Sham Sells 1 lot	1	1
2	John Buys 3 lots Tom Sells 3 lots	3	4
3	Ram Sells his 1 lot Tom Buys 1 lot	-1	3

On the fourth day, San buys 3 lots, and John sells his 3 lots.
After the fourth day:

Day	Activity	OI Change	Total OI
1	Ram Buys 1 lot Sham Sells 1 lot	1	1
2	John Buys 3 lots Tom Sells 3 lots	3	4
3	Ram Sells his 1 lot Tom Buys 1 lot	-1	3
4	San Buys 3 lots John Sells his 3 lots	0	3

Whenever a buyer and seller initiate a new position, the OI count will increase by 1. Similarly, when both of them close their position, the OI count will decrease by 1.

But when a buyer or seller passes their existing position to a new person, the OI count remains unchanged (but the volume count increases in this case).

Compared to OI, volume count will be added every time, irrespective of old or new player participation.

Day	Activity	OI Change	Total OI	Volume
1	Ram Buys 1 lot Sham Sells 1 lot	1	1	1
2	John Buys 3 lots Tom Sells 3 lots	3	4	4
3	Ram Sells his 1 lot Tom Buys 1 lot	-1	3	5
4	San Buys 3 lots John Sells his 3 lots	0	3	8

This example shows how OI can give you a better idea of market liquidity than volume. Even though the volume was higher on the third and fourth days, the OI dropped, meaning fewer future lots were being traded.

On the other hand, volume is simply a measure of how many future lots are traded. It doesn't give you any information about how many future lots are actually available to be traded (that is, OI).

For this reason, OI is often used as a measure of market liquidity, while volume is used as a measure of market activity.

How to Interpret OI with Futures Price?

When OI increases, it means that more contracts are being traded, and there is more participation in the market. This usually indicates that prices are moving in a particular direction and because of momentum.

Conversely, when OI decreases, it means that fewer contracts are being traded, and there is less participation in the market. This usually indicates that prices are range-bound or consolidating.

OI can be used to gauge market sentiment and confirm price movements. If prices rise and OI increases, this is a bullish sign.

Image 12.6 shows an example where the price increased along with an increase in OI. This indicates that the market participants are interested in holding their long position as they anticipate further price increases.

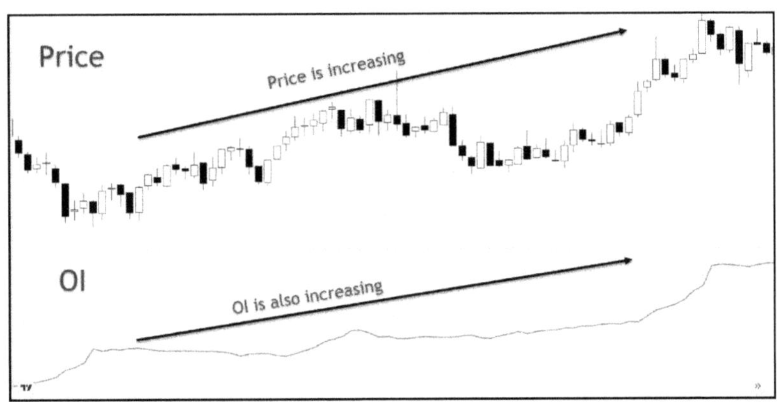

Image 12.6: Price and OI increasing (bullish)

If prices are falling and OI increases, this is a bearish sign (image 12.7). The above image shows an example of this scenario.

The increase in OI and a fall in price indicate the active interests of short players who are holding their position, anticipating a further fall.

When the price increases with a decrease in OI (image 12.8), it indicates the absence of big players (their presence will increase the OI).

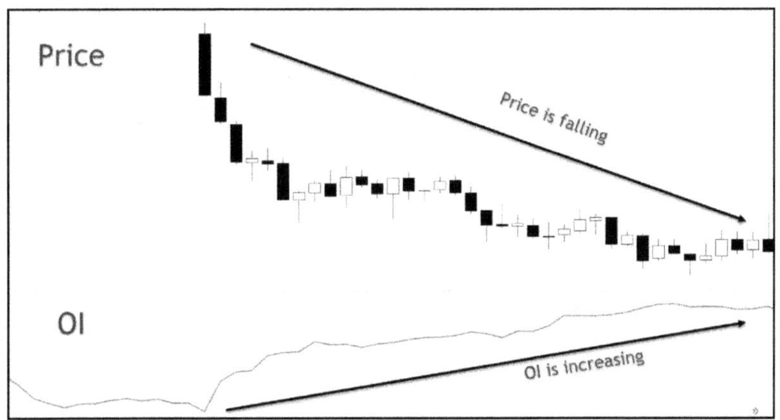

Image 12.7: Price is falling, but OI is increasing (bearish)

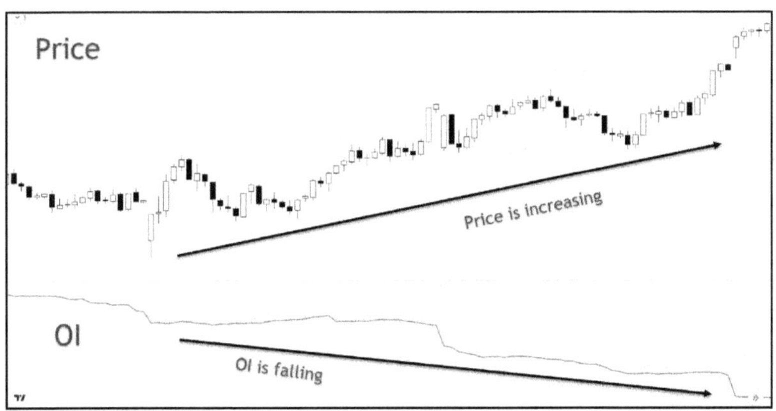

Image 12.8: Price is increasing, but OI is falling (short covering)

It indicates the short covering from the small traders, who were holding some short positions anticipating a fall. So, we can maintain a sideways to bullish view in this case.

When the price falls with a decrease in OI (image 12.9), it indicates the absence of big players (their presence will increase the OI). It indicates the long unwinding from the small traders,

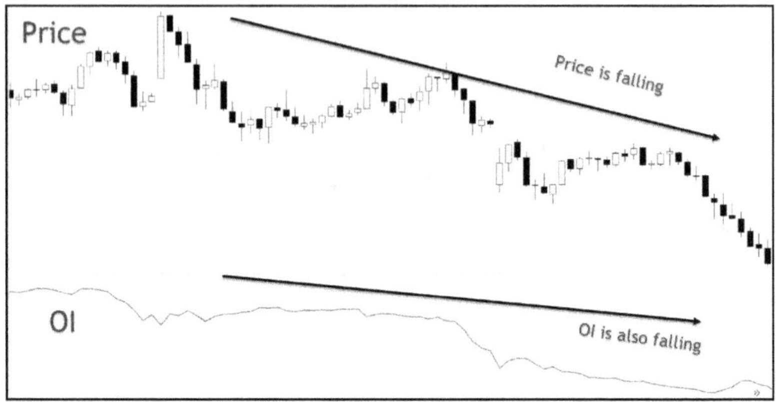

Image 12.9: Price is falling, OI is also falling (long unwinding)

who were holding long positions anticipating a price rise. So, we can maintain a sideways to bearish view in this case.

HOW TO IDENTIFY SUPPORT AND RESISTANCE LEVELS USING OPEN INTEREST

When it comes to finding support and resistance levels, one of the newest and most innovative methods traders use is to look at OI. It represents the number of currently open and active contracts in a market.

OI can be helpful in finding these levels because it can give you an idea of where there is likely to be more buying or selling pressure.

Suppose there is a lot of open interest at a certain price level. In that case, it stands to reason that there is likely to be more trading activity taking place there.

This increased activity can either push the price higher (if there is more buying pressure) or lower (if there is more selling pressure).

ABB stock is trading CMP at 3260.90 (image 12.10).

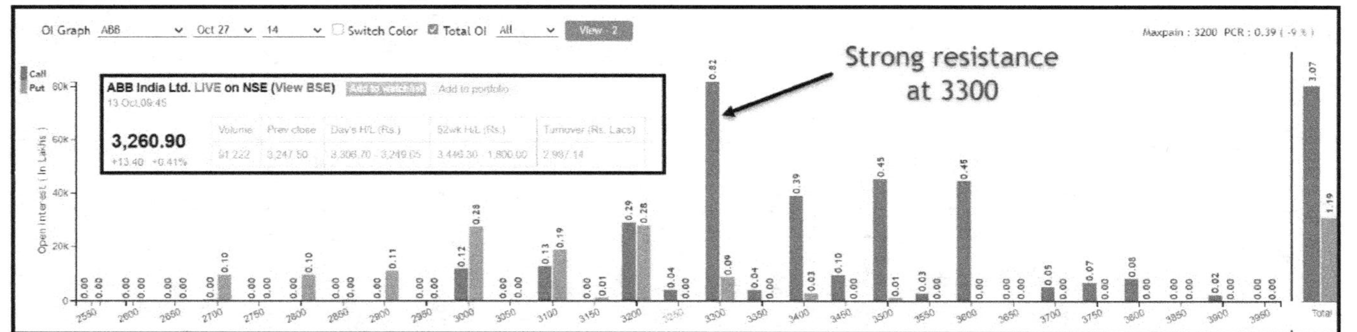

Image 12.10: Resistance identification using OI in ABB

There is massive selling of CE at a 3300 price (over 83K). It indicates that the big players sold lots of 3300 CE to collect the premium. It denotes that the big players are not expecting a rise above 3300 this month. If the price comes near 3300, they try to defend their position (either by shorting futures or selling equity, etc.).

Hence 3300 level acts as a strong resistance for ABB this month.

Adani Enterprises stock is trading CMP at 3230.45 (image 12.11).

But there is massive selling of PE at a 3000 price. It indicates that the big players sold lots of 3000 PE to collect the premium. Further, it indicates that the big players are not expecting a fall below 3000 this month. If the price falls near 3000, they prevent the fall by buying equity or futures.

Hence 3000 level acts as a strong support for Adani Enterprises this month.

When trading any financial instrument, it is crucial to know the potential risks involved. OI can be used as a guide to market activity. However, it is essential to remember that it does not necessarily reflect the total amount of cash flowing into or out of a contract.

There are a few things to keep in mind when using OI as an indicator:

1. OI can increase even if the price remains unchanged–this happens when new contracts are created, but old ones are not closed.
2. OI can decrease even if the price remains unchanged–this happens when old contracts are closed, but new ones are not created.
3. It can be misleading in a thinly traded contract–a small number of trades can significantly impact OI.

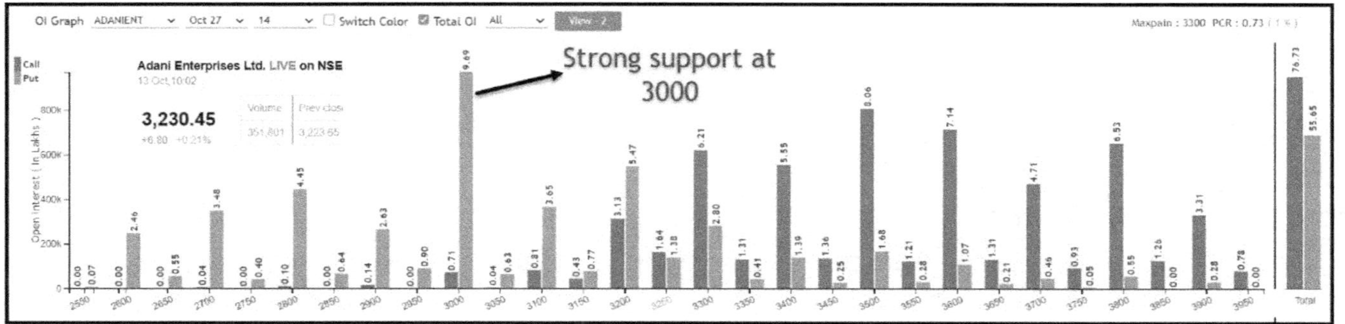

Image 12.11: Support identification using OI in Adani Enterprises

4. OI can be affected by the expiration of contracts. As contracts approach their expiration date, there is often a surge in activity as traders close or roll over their positions.
5. It can be affected by holidays and other events that cause trading to slow down or stop entirely.

OI can be a helpful tool for traders when used correctly. However, it is essential to remember that open interest is just an indication of data and should not be relied upon exclusively. It is better to sync with any trading setup you have.

13

THE BEST WAYS TO HANDLE STRESS WHEN YOU TRADE ALONE

Stress is an unavoidable part of stock market trading. Even the most experienced traders can be overwhelmed by the fast pace and ever-changing dynamics of the markets.

The market often moves in unexpected directions, making it difficult for traders to make informed decisions about their trades. Traders also face the constant risk of loss associated with each transaction, which can cause significant stress levels if not managed properly.

The fear of losing money due to high volatility or bad decision-making can increase traders' stress levels. As such, they may become emotionally attached to certain positions or feel overwhelmed when making decisions that could potentially result in a significant loss.

They are also at risk of experiencing 'trading fatigue'–feeling exhausted due to long trading hours and the pressure to make profitable decisions.

Overall, stress is an unavoidable part of stock market trading. However, with the right strategies and self-care measures, traders

can manage their stress levels and remain focused on making profitable decisions.

It is also worth noting that while making losses may be inevitable at times, it should not prevent traders from pursuing their goals or cause them to abandon their chosen strategies.

By taking these steps to manage stress levels and stay disciplined, traders can maximize their chances of success in the markets.

1. Don't Take Trading as a Full-time Career in the Beginning

Many beginners commit the mistake of taking trading as their full-time career when they make some profits initially. Due to beginner's luck, most beginners make some initial profits, and it makes them feel that trading is easy and money can be made easily in this process.

Anyone can learn trading or investment when they have a proper day job or business, as there is no pressure to generate some monthly returns to pay the bills.

It may be tempting to dive in first and start trading your entire portfolio, but this is usually a recipe for disaster. Instead, start small and gradually increase your exposure as you gain experience and confidence.

Also, ensure you have a solid plan before starting out. This will help keep you calm and focused when the markets get tough.

2. Don't Aim to Make Millions in Every Trade

Most people aim for big profits with each trade. There are only two ways to make big profits:

1. Price should move big in the trade direction, or
2. Take a big position so that even a small position in the expected direction will give good profits.

Nevertheless, option 1 is not in our control, and option 2 can wipe out your entire capital in a few trades.

As I said, do not aim for huge profits in every single trade. It is impossible to make big profits in every trade; it will only lead to stress and frustration.

Instead, one should focus on making small, consistent profits over time. This will help you stay calm and in control while trading and lead to a more relaxed and enjoyable experience.

Also, try to find a trading system that works well for you and stick with it. Do not change your system every time you have a bad trade, it will only add to your stress. Instead, analyze what went wrong with the trade and learn from it to improve your trading skills in the future.

3. Develop the Ability to Digest Failures

When we grow up, our parents, relatives, and neighbors suggest scoring good marks and saying that failure is pathetic in education. This repeated advice from those close to us acts as affirmation, and we store 'failure is bad' logic in our subconscious mind.

So in most cases, when we face failure, we take it to heart, and most of us try to correct it immediately by taking some action.

When it comes to the stock market, nobody can get 100% accuracy with their trades, and some failed trades are part of the trading business.

However, because of the 'failure is bad' thought process, when we face a failed trade, we end up taking many unnecessary trades or more risk per trade (or a combination of both).

The stock market is a volatile place, and you will inevitably experience some losses along the way. The key to success is to develop the ability to digest your failures, learn from them, and move on. Please do not dwell on your mistakes, and do not let them affect your future trading decisions.

Remember that nobody has a perfect track record in the market—even the most successful traders experience losses from time to time.

Stay calm and focused when trading, and remember that losing money is part of the game. If you can keep a level head during times of stress, you will be more likely to make rational trading decisions that could lead to financial success.

4. Develop and Follow a Proper Trade Plan

A well-developed trade plan will help you manage your emotions and remain calm under pressure. It can also help you make better, more informed trading decisions.

Some key points to keep in mind when developing your trade plan:

- **O** Define your goals and risk tolerance.
- **O** Choose the right trading strategy for you.
- **O** Create a realistic schedule and stick to it.
- **O** Use stop-losses to limit losses and protect profits.
- **O** Always use limit orders to enter or exit positions.
- **O** Stay disciplined, patient, and focused.

5. Anything Can Happen in the Market

Let us assume all the world markets are bullish. The entire segment is bullish, and the stock you have invested within that segment is bullish.

Now, you think there is no way this stock can go down.

However, do you know what will happen to that price if a country starts or announces a war?

There is a high probability that the stock's price will go down. Always remember that anything can happen in the market anytime.

As I mentioned before, no one can predict the stock market with 100% accuracy, so it's essential to always be prepared for anything. Volatility can happen anytime, so ensure you are keeping a close eye on your trades and have a backup plan ready in case things go wrong.

Stay calm and make intelligent decisions based on the available information.

6. Always Keep Stop-loss for Each Trade

Always keep a stop-loss for each trade. This will help to ensure that you do not lose more money than you are willing to, and it will help to keep your stress levels low.

When you are in the heat of the moment, it can be difficult to make rational decisions. That is why it's crucial to have a system that clearly defines the stop-loss rule in place that will help you stay disciplined.

If something goes wrong, do not beat yourself up; learn from your mistakes and move on. Remember that stock market trading is a learning process, and there are no guarantees. Stay calm and collected, and always use stop losses to protect your capital.

7. Don't Look at Profit Screenshots of Other Traders

Ask yourself these questions when you see a big profit screenshot of other traders:

1. Does it teach any trading skills?
2. Does it teach any money management rules?
3. Does it calm my mind?

If the answer is 'yes' to any of these questions, then it makes sense to consider that profit screenshot seriously. However, a big profit screenshot can only trigger the 'greed' part of your emotions, and you end up taking many unwanted trades with more risk.

One of the most common ways to get stressed in stock market trading is to look at the profits or losses of other traders. When you see that someone has made a killing in a day, it can make you feel like you are missing out and stressed. But when you see that someone has lost money, it can make you feel anxious and worried.

Remember that everyone has different strategies and that there is no right way to trade stocks. So do not compare your performance to others–focus on your own goals and strategies. In addition, if you do start feeling overwhelmed or stressed, take a break and walk away from the computer.

Overall, stock market trading can be a stressful activity due to its ever-changing environment and the potential risks associated with it. Therefore, traders must remain mindful of their emotions and take steps to manage any related stress they may experience while trading to ensure long-term success.

14

The Shocking Revelation of Different Stages of Trading

I started exploring the stock market in 2008–9. The Indian market was in a significant uptrend after the 2008 global recession.

Back then, I had just started my career in IT, and observed all actions of my colleagues in the market.

Intraday was not that widespread in the absence of discount brokers, and most engaged in either positional trading or BTST trading.

I would sit quietly when my colleagues discussed stock market ideas. Besides, I also made a habit of reading 2–3 financial newspapers before the market opened.

I felt a little confident and started taking small positional trades. Some were successful, and I lost money in others.

In 2009, the Satyam scam broke out (India's biggest corporate fraud), and Satyam shares fell drastically (from 400 to 6 or 7).

During a coffee break, one of my colleagues told us that the Government of India (GOI) would not keep quiet as lakhs of Satyam employees would become jobless if it allowed the company to sink.

So, his gut feeling was that GOI would take over the company soon. If it happened, the share value of Satyam would skyrocket.

This explanation made sense to me, and Satyam shares were trading for around 10–15 rupees at the time.

I had decent capital in my trading account. So, I bought Satyam shares using all the capital.

After a few days of my investment, it was announced that another big Indian company, Mahindra would take over Satyam.

So, the price of Satyam shares started going north. I began booking profits in multiple slots whenever the price went upside.

Finally, **I made 7–8 times returns on my capital.**

I felt like a scientist who discovered something that was unknown to the entire world, and I chose not to share my secret to make massive money in the market.

This phase is called **beginners luck.**

It brings a beautiful illusion in the beginners' minds that trading is effortless and that they are smart to make profits in trading.

Image 12.1: Beginners luck phase

After making huge profits from Satyam's scandal, I believed making money in trading was easy. So, I made a clear plan to execute it.

My plan:

1. Find the shares that fell over 80–90% of their value in the last month.
2. Invest only 5–10% capital per trade.
3. Not all trades give profits. But I assumed 25–50% of trades would result in profits.
4. Once the stock starts going upwards, book profit in multiple intervals.
5. Repeat 1–4 steps and make huge profits.

I started to implement these steps rigorously in the next two months. After two months, not only did I lose all the profits I made from the Satyam scandal, but I also lost the original capital.

This is the **losses phase.**

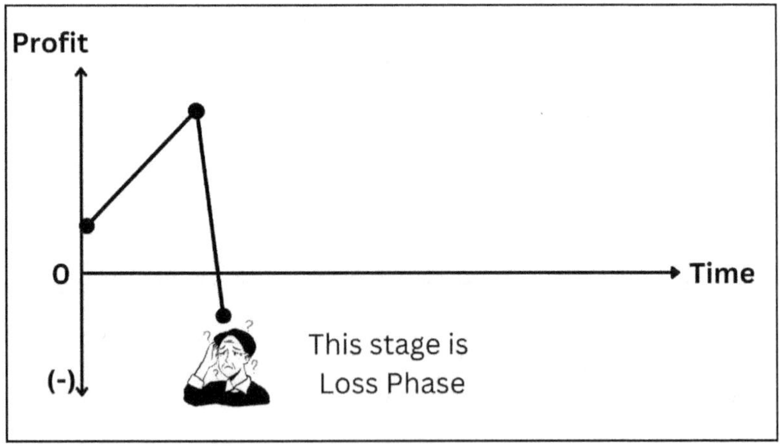

Image 12.2: Loss phase in trading

At this stage, traders realize earning profits from the market is not that easy, and it demands a lot of effort, skill, and discipline to succeed in the market.

This is an interesting phase where the trader is trying to learn everything they can about the stock market. It involves reading books, taking courses, and doing research to understand how the stock market works. I also attended a few trading workshops and read books about the stock market. Most of my weekends were dedicated to knowing more about the stock market.

Even though I gained some confidence, there was some fear in my mind after facing the loss. Yet, I decided to go ahead to take some trades.

I was utterly shocked during this phase because most of my trades failed. If I took a long trade, the price would return and hit the stop-loss. If I took an opposite short trade, the price again would hit the stop-loss and went upside. I was literally clueless.

This is the **more losses phase.**

In this stage, most traders think it is impossible to make profits in trading, and they quit the game (at least for some time).

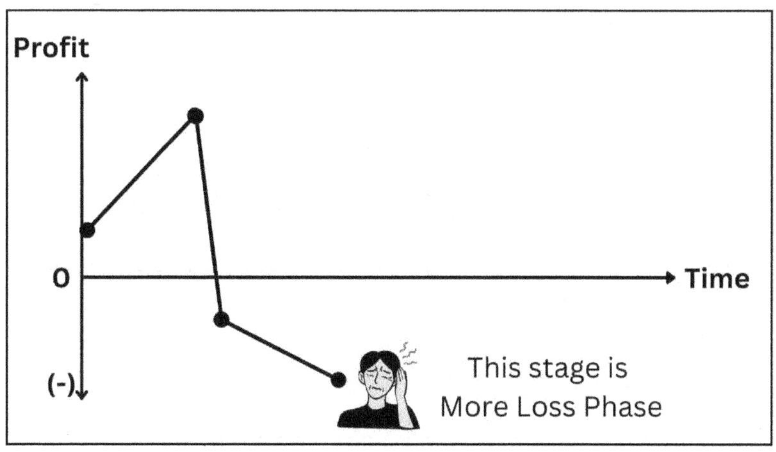

Image 12.3: More loss phase in trading

I was disappointed during this phase and quit trading for a few months. I stopped reading newspapers and trading books. Besides, I didn't attend any workshops for a few months.

But after a gap of a few months, once again, I started trading activities. I realized there is no holy grail in trading, and it all depends on the system with a positive edge, money management rules, and good trading psychology to succeed in trading.

So, I developed a simple intraday trading system based on the stochastic indicator. Usually, the stochastic indicator is used as an overbought and oversold indicator (80 and 20 rule).

But the same stochastic indicator can stay above 80 in an uptrend and stay below 20 in a downtrend.

I used to take long trades in Nifty whenever the stochastic broke above 80 in the 15-minute chart and short trades when the stochastic broke below 20. Even in this phase, I committed some mistakes because of the earlier losses and fear of missing out. However, my losses reduced drastically compared to the previous phase.

This is **less losses phase.**

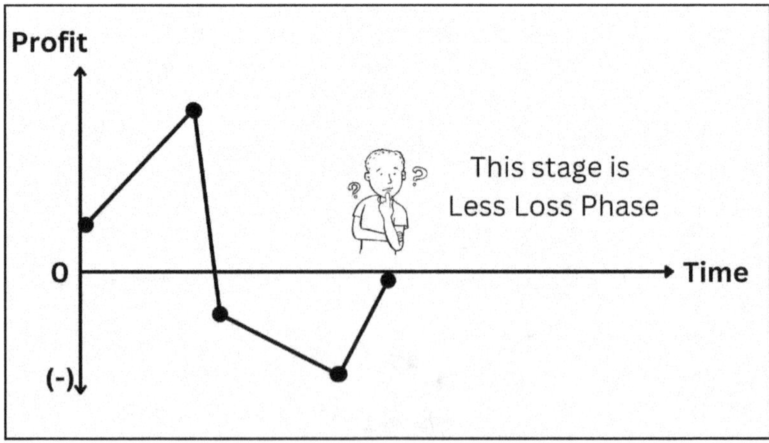

Image 12.4: Less loss phase in trading

In this phase, most traders see little hope in trading. But because of their past experiences, they still commit some mistakes.

While going through this phase, I discussed this issue with my mentor.

He suggested logging all the trades every day. He asked me to come back once I had 40–50 failed trades.

I reached out to him after 50 failed trades. He noticed a major pattern with all the losing trades. Around 80% of these losing trades came when I felt bad after facing 1–2 failures on a trading day, and I took these revenge trades to get back my money from the market.

He came up with a simple solution in the form of 2 rules:

1. Don't take trades when faced with 2 failed trades on any trading day, and
2. Don't take more than 3 trades on any trading day.

It was not easy to follow these rules in the live market. So, I used to close my trading terminal in such situations.

Once in a while, I broke the rules and took further trades. Still, these rules helped me avoid my revenge trades.

This is **breakeven phase** (no loss and no profit).

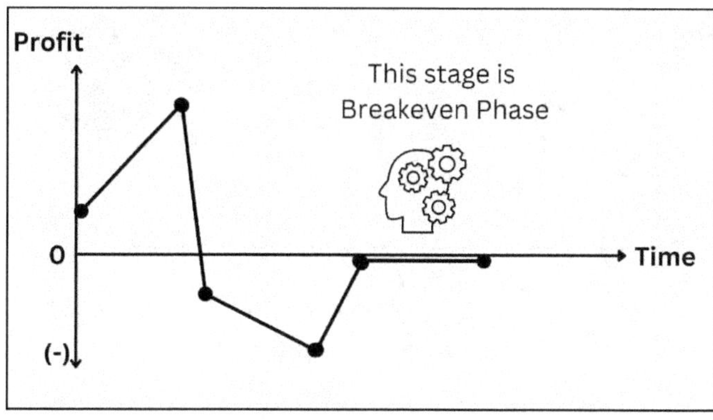

Image 12.5: Breakeven phase in trading

In this phase, traders realize success is very close to them.

This was the most frustrating phase of my trading career. I stayed in this phase for 6–7 months, which was an emotionally draining experience.

I took trades almost daily (intraday trades) but did not make any profits or lose any money (breakeven).

During this period, I didn't make the earlier mistake of revenge trading, but, I was still unable to make profits. In retrospect, I realized that I could not hold winning trades for a long time and booked profits early most of the time.

I came up with a simple solution to counter this. I would book profit only for 50% of the position and started carrying the remaining 50% with my entry price as a stop-loss.

I immediately saw some profits after practicing this for one month. This gave me the confidence and conviction to carry my winning trades.

Not all traders experience the same phases in their trading careers. Some people are smart, and they quickly get into the winning phase. But common people like us will go through a similar experience.

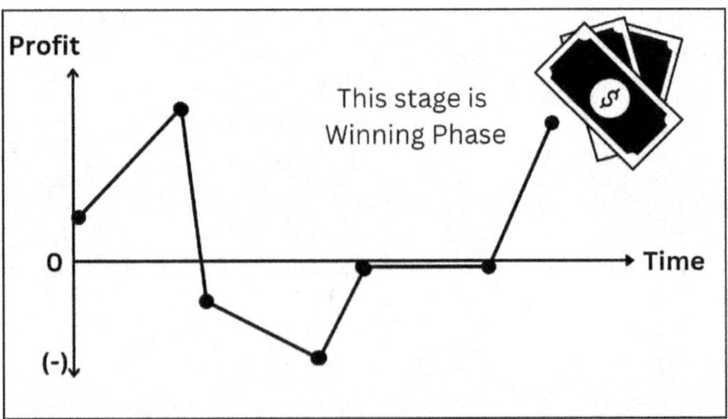

Image 12.6: Winning phase in trading

It takes a lot of hard work and dedication to be successful in trading. You need to have a strong understanding of the markets and know what you are doing.

There is no room for error when you are trading. You also need to be able to handle the stress that comes with trading. It can be very stressful sometimes, but you will probably not be successful if you can't take it.

There are a lot of people who are not successful in trading because they crumble under pressure. So, if you want to be successful in trading, you need to be able to take the pressure.

Glossary

ADX Indicator - ADX is a technical indicator that measures the strength of a particular trend in a scrip. The ADX indicator can be used to help traders determine whether a market is trending or not, as well as the strength of that trend.

Algorithmic (algo) Trading - Algorithmic trading is a simple method of executing trading orders (buy or sell) using automated pre-programmed trading instructions to send orders whenever some criteria are satisfied.

Average True Range (ATR) – It is a technical indicator developed by J Welles Wilder Jr, which is used to measure the volatility.

Bollinger Band – It is a type of technical indicator that is used to measure the volatility in a scrip. It consists of three different lines – 1) A 20-period SMA as middle line and 2) Two lines as two standard deviations (SD) above and below the middle line.

Breakout Trading – It is a simple trading technique that involves buying of scrips when the price moves outside of a resistance zone with increased volume.

FII – Foreign Institutional Investors (an individual investor or big investing firm located in some other country, but investing in India).

Futures and Options - Futures and options are two popular derivative trading instruments frequently used by traders and investors to manage risk or speculate on the future direction of an underlying asset. Futures contracts give the buyer the obligation to purchase a certain quantity of an underlying asset at a specified price on a predetermined date in the future. On the other hand, options give the holder the right, but not the obligation, to buy or sell an asset at a predetermined price on a specified date in the future.

Indicator Based Trading – It is a trading technique in which traders use one or multiple technical indicators to make the trading decision.

Intraday Trading – It is also called day trading in which traders close their position on the same day (buy and sell on the same day).

Mean Reversion - A strategy that aims to buy when an asset price is lower and then seeks to sell it on the next higher bounce.

Momentum Trading – It is a trading strategy that involves trading a scrip which received significant movement in price or increase in volume.

Multi-bagger Stocks – A common term used to indicate the stocks which gives a return of more than 100%.

Parabolic SAR (PSAR) Indicator – This is a technical indicator that consists of a series of dots above or below the price candles. It will appear below the price candle if the stock is in an uptrend and above the price candle if it is in a downtrend.

PIP - It stands for percentage in point. It is the smallest unit price in a forex trading instrument.

Position Sizing - It is nothing but the quantity of scrip one buys (or sells) in one trade. It is calculated using the formula:

$$Position\ Size = Risk\ per\ Trade\ /\ Stop\text{-}loss$$

Price Action Trading - It is a trading technique in which traders read the chart, and make subjective trading decisions based on the price movements, rather than relying on technical indicators. In simple words, traders use only 'Price' and 'Volume' to make any trading decision.

Relative Strength Index (RSI) - It is a momentum oscillator indicator used that measures the magnitude (both speed and change) of recent price changes.

Short Position in equities – This is a regulatory requirement to avoid any insider trading. At the time of writing this book (2023), naked short selling is not permitted in the Indian stock market.

Smallcase – It is a company that provides various diversified investment products at less cost.

Swing Trading - Swing trading is a trading technique that seeks to capture a swing when the price goes to a complete sideways zone.

Trading Setup – Traders study several chart patterns and rely on one chart pattern to increase the probability of winning.

www.ingramcontent.com/pod-product-compliance
Lightning Source LLC
LaVergne TN
LVHW050901200726
843508LV00011B/2072